For Maivn Sharples

Peter Passell

THE BEST
☆ ENCORE ☆

PETER PASSELL

Illustrations by KIMBLE MEAD

FARRAR, STRAUS AND GIROUX   NEW YORK

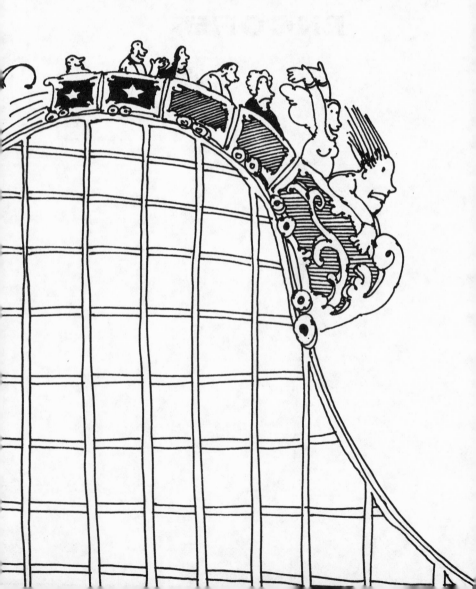

THE BEST
☆ ENCORE ☆

Text copyright © 1977 by Peter Passell
Illustrations copyright © 1977 by Kimble Mead
All rights reserved
Printed in the United States of America
Published simultaneously in Canada
by McGraw-Hill Ryerson Ltd., Toronto
Designed by Marion Hess
First edition, 1977
Portions of the text originally appeared in *Esquire*

Library of Congress Cataloging in Publication Data
Passell, Peter. The best, encore.
1. Consumer education.   2. Curiosities and wonders.
I. Title.
TX335.P36   1977   031'.02   77–2894

THE BEST
☆ ENCORE ☆

THE BEST AMERICAN CHAMPAGNE

True champagne comes from a few thousand acres of vineyards in northeastern France. While German, Italian, and Spanish sparkling wine makers fear retaliation sufficiently to stay off French turf, dozens of American vineyards label their bubbly white wines champagne. Ironically, me-too-ism has proved a handicap: the most faithful copies are overpriced failures, while the very best American champagnes hardly resemble their Gallic namesakes.

Almost all domestic champagne—certainly all you would want to drink—is made in New York and California. Cheaper brews, the stuff under four dollars, spend their youth in steel tanks soaking up carbon dioxide bubbles from secondary fermentation and are then filtered and bottled under pressure. These "bulk" or Charmat process fizzies are real enough (it's illegal to carbonate champagne artificially), but no one has figured out a way to make them very tasty. New York bulk-process champagnes invariably resemble Welch's grape juice, the mark of the native East Coast *labrusca* grape family. By contrast, California bulk-process is typically quite bland, a result of using cheap high-yield grapes grown in the state's Central Valley. Probably the inexpensive California champagne with the most character is Gallo; New York bargain brands have far too much character . . .

Expensive champagnes from both states grow their own bubbles in the bottle. But this isn't the sole difference. French champagnes are made only from Pinot Chardonnay and Pinot Noir; if only the paler, more delicate Chardonnay grape is used, the finished product may be labeled "Blanc de Blancs." Other high-quality grape varietals find their way into better American champagne: in California, the blend may include Riesling or Sauvignon Blanc; in New York, hybrid grapes free of the *labrusca* tang.

Virtually all champagne is sweetened with sugar syrup before it's corked for the last time. There's nothing disreputable about the practice; sugar cuts the harsh edge found in most naturally finished champagne. The quantity of sugar needed to eliminate this harshness varies considerably, however, and if too much must be added the wine loses subtlety. Hence the best champagnes are dry. Almost all expensive champagnes are labeled "Brut," though in practice this can mean anything from faintly sweet to extremely dry. In the doublethink of the wine industry, "Extra Dry" translates as sweet and "Demi Sec" will give you cavities.

A few American champagnes have started marking vintages—mostly, no doubt, to justify inflated prices. We don't approve, even in theory. Blending is crucial to all sparkling

4

wine production, and it doesn't make sense to limit vintners to a single harvest. French champagne suffers from the economic pressure to declare a "vintage" year when blending would make better wine.

Herewith the rankings, the best first. A few good California champagnes have been left out because they are rarely available outside thirty or forty wine stores in the state. (None, incidentally, is better than Korbel Natural.)

Korbel Natural—Medium-dry and very flavorful. A fuller-bodied wine than any expensive French Brut. As the word *natural* in the name suggests, no sugar has been added. This is only possible, we suspect, because the grape blend includes Sauvignon.

Hanns Kornell Brut—Less full-bodied and lighter in color than Korbel Natural. The very nice flavor is slightly marred by a hint of bitterness in the aftertaste.

Schramsberg Blanc de Blancs—The most ambitious (and, at eleven dollars, the most expensive) California champagne. Very pale, very dry, very subtle. Nixon put Schramsberg on the map by hauling several cases to the Orient and using it to toast Chairman Mao. Unfortunately it doesn't taste all that good—an elegant failure.

Gold Seal Blanc de Blancs—By far the best New York champagne. Quite dry; a touch bitter. Demolishes the plebian reputation of New York State champagnes.

Korbel Brut—Very similar to Korbel Natural, but slightly sweeter and less interesting. It's okay, but no bargain at only a dollar less than the Natural.

Almadén Blanc de Blancs—Passably bubbly, but the flavor seems washed out, as if the wine were diluted with some chemically mineral water.

Paul Masson Brut—Pleasant, but dull. Like Korbel Brut, a shade too sweet to complement unsweetened food.

Almadén Brut—A waste of money. Flat, boring taste reminiscent of better bulk-process champagnes.

Taylor Brut and *Great Western Brut*—Both are unable to mask an unmistakable whiff of Concord. Like Twinkies and Velveeta, a taste most easily acquired before the age of ten.

• THE BEST ANNIVERSARY PRESENT FOR MARGAUX HEMINGWAY WETSON

Asprey and Co., Ltd., of Bond Street, London, recently created a solid gold french fry (crinkle-cut) for an unidentified customer. The same client also ordered a sterling-silver club sandwich (sliced egg garnish), but Ms. Hemingway might prefer a double cheeseburger, hold the onions.

• THE BEST ANSWER TO HOW I KNEW OUR TRUE LOVE WAS THROUGH

When the smoke gets in your eyes, argued General Motors recently, in response to a call for auto safety improvements. GM catalytic converters have a nasty habit of overheating if they are attached to the exhausts of poorly tuned engines, so the National Highway Traffic Safety Administration queried the giant auto manufacturer on the desirability of installing a warning light on the dash.

GM demurred, adding that the company had already built in a "unique warning to the driver":

"Decreased driveability usually precedes any detectable olfactory or visual sensations. If the driver continues to ignore the poor driveability, a pungent odor from the hot body sealer is noticeable for about two minutes. About two minutes following the odor detection, light smoke emanates from around the edges of the carpet. At about five minutes the smoke increases in intensity to the extent that the eyes and throat become irritated. At about seven minutes the level of irritation is very extreme and exit from the vehicle is required. . . . Unlike other types of warning systems, this one could not be overlooked by the operator of the vehicles."

• THE BEST ANTACID

If you think choosing a good antacid is as simple as spelling "relief," think again. Many of the tummy potions displayed on drugstore shelves—including nearly all the heavily advertised ones—are either ineffective or hazardous, or both.

First, a short lecture from Mr. Wizard. Antacids are just what they sound like: chemicals that neutralize natural stomach acid. Now, acid is absolutely necessary for digestion, but if too much of it is secreted, say after a toasted almond fudge orgy or a look at the Consumer Price Index, the stomach begins to digest itself. A dozen chemicals do a fair job of slaking the fires. The trick is to find one that is cheap, has no important side effects, and doesn't taste like the White Cliffs of Dover.

The most commonly used antacid is probably sodium bicarbonate, the active ingredient in Alka-Seltzer, Bromo Seltzer, and Brioschi. Sodium bicarbonate works fast and is easy on the palate. It is also dangerous for a lot of people. A single dose per day can ruin an otherwise successful low-salt diet, the keystone to the control (and possibly the prevention) of high blood pressure. Regular use of bicarbonates has also been linked to kidney disease and other uncharming afflictions. Worse yet, some manufacturers of bicarbonate antacids add other drugs—aspirin, caffeine—to the brew, drugs that have no positive effect on indigestion and may add a whole extra dimension of side effects. The FDA is considering a crackdown on such compounds, but don't count the days until the feds save you from your ignorance.

The next most popular antacid, calcium carbonate, found in Tums and Alka 2, scores a bit better than sodium bicarbonate. It works very quickly, and as the ads say, every little tablet neutralizes a lot of acid. While few people actually find calcium carbonate pleasant to chew (it's an acquired taste), most prefer it to the alternatives. One study has found, however, that calcium carbonate creates a rebound effect, first neutralizing acid, then stimulating the production of more acid. Add the side effects of constipation and possible kidney damage from long-term use, and we think calcium carbonate flunks.

This leaves two standard antacids: magnesium hydroxide and aluminum hydroxide. Neither is perfect. Straight magnesium compounds (Milk of Magnesia) can cause diarrhea, while straight aluminum compounds can be constipating. And both are no-nos for kidney-ailment sufferers. By blending the two, though, it's possible to finesse the intestinal pitfalls. Brand names of choice include Maalox, Gelusil, Mylanta, and Di-Gel. Note, however, that Di-Gel and Mylanta also contain simethicone to relieve gas pains. Simethicone is unlikely to do you any damage, but its effect on gas pains is unproven.

Whatever antacid you take, the liquid version generally is more effective than tablets, since few people have the patience to chew them thoroughly. One striking exception to the rule is Pepto-Bismol. Pepto-Bismol tablets are mainly calcium carbonate. But the nice pink P-B liquid contains no antacid at all. Its active ingredient is bismuth subsalicylate, an inefficient pain reliever.

A last word: antacids are medicine. If you are healthy you shouldn't need them very often. If the food you eat is rotten, change cooks. If antacids are just a nervous habit, switch to Trident or take up needlepoint.

• **THE BEST ARMED FORCE IN THE MIDEAST**
Here's the top of the pecking order, as of late 1976. Barring another war, the relative strengths of the prime combatants should remain stable for several years, or until one of the major powers chooses to upset the balance.

No. 1:   Israel. Contrary to common belief, Israel did not lose the 1973 war on the battlefield. After initial heavy losses of tanks and ground-support aircraft, it regained the advantage against Syria in the Golan Heights and was in a position to decimate the Egyptian Army west of the Suez when Soviet and American political pressure forced a truce. The Israeli Defense Force retains an edge over the combined Arab military—a very substantial edge were Israel to strike first.

Military superiority does not come cheaply. Israel spends $4 billion on defense annually, one third of its GNP. This permanent war footing has seriously damaged the Israeli economy, leaving it with the world's highest taxes, grave inflation, and a persistent foreign trade deficit. Regular military personnel total about 150,000, but another 250,000 (nearly 10 percent of the population) can be mobilized within seventy-two hours. The steel backbone of

Israel's military capability is some 600 fighter-interceptor and attack-support planes, 3,000-plus medium tanks, and a Hawk surface-to-air missile defense system. On paper the Israeli Air Force and Army are neither as large nor as modern as the enemy's, but this disadvantage is overcome by an enormous logistic advantage and superior training and tactical leadership.

Israel manufactures a high-quality battle tank of its own, the Sabra, and a Mach 2 fighter-bomber, the Kfir. It remains dependent on sophisticated U.S. missile technology to sustain parity with the Arabs, and would be totally dependent on U.S. resupply of tanks and planes in any future 1973-style war of attrition.

No. 2: Egypt. A massive and increasingly capable military force, whose morale has been high since the Suez Canal crossing in October 1973. Egypt maintains a huge army, 325,000 under arms with another 500,000 in the reserves. More important, the defense budget tops $6 billion, spent mostly on super-modern Soviet armor and combat aircraft.

The air force can boast of 350 MiG-21's, with about 50 MiG-23's (the main-line Warsaw Pact fighter) and 90 French state-of-the-art Mirage F-1 fighters on the way. Saudi Arabia and Kuwait are footing the bill for the F-1's, their token in support of the liberation of Jerusalem. Egypt's 2,000-tank army consists of about half T-54/55's and half T-62's, the Soviet medium tanks of the 1960's and 1970's, respectively. High-altitude reconnaissance is probably performed by Russian pilots flying MiG-25's, a task undoubtedly handled for Israel by U.S. Air Force SR-71's.

No. 3: Syria. The Syrian Baathist regime has almost as many enemies as Israel: apart from its formidable foe on the Golan Heights, there are the rival Baathist party in Iraq, the Palestinians, leftist Muslims in Lebanon, and (from time to time) Jordan.

Its tough, but overextended, military force relies heavily on 2,000 medium Russian tanks (two thirds T-54/55's, one third T-62's), which performed so well against Israel in 1973 and so badly against the Lebanese Left in 1976. The air force has at least 250 MiG-21's and 45 MiG-23's, the latter quite possibly flown in combat by Soviet pilots.

No. 4: Iran. The Shah spent more on armaments in 1976 than Egypt and Israel combined. Iran is buying 80 F14 Grumman Tomcats (the world's most advanced fighter-interceptor), 160 General Dynamics F16 fighters, 205 Phantoms, 180 Northrop F-5 Tiger lightweight fighters, 56 C-130 Hercules turboprop transports, 250 British Scorpion lightweight tanks, 1,700 British Chieftain medium-weight battle tanks, 3 attack submarines, and 6 destroyers to beef up its current supply of 100 Phantoms, 140 Tigers, 55 Hercules, 1,300 medium-weight tanks, and 3 destroyers.

Nominally, all this firepower is to protect Iran from the Soviet bear hug. More likely, it's meant to intimidate Iraq and to keep Saudi Arabia's hands away from the oil that probably lies undiscovered offshore in the Persian Gulf. It will be at least five years before Iranian personnel can keep all the computers working without U.S. assistance. But then, watch Iran go . . .

• THE BEST ART MUSEUM IN AMERICA

If having more of everything is what counts, that great warehouse of art the Metropolitan Museum in New York must be the best, followed (distantly) by D.C.'s National

Gallery. Among specialized collections, the Museum of Modern Art in New York has no peer, though oriental art is superbly represented in the little-known Freer Gallery in Washington. In another category entirely are smaller family collections, opened to the public for reasons of philanthropy or inheritance taxes: the Barnes Foundation outside Philadelphia, the Hill-Stead Museum in Farmington, Connecticut, the Frick Collection in New York. And for those who care more about what a museum looks like than what it contains, there are, of course, New York's Guggenheim (Frank Lloyd Wright), Pittsburgh's Scaife Gallery (E. L. Barnes), Houston's Brown Pavilion (Mies van der Rohe), Ithaca's Cornell Museum (I. M. Pei), not to mention John Paul Getty's imperial Roman villa in Malibu.

Our choice, however, is neither the biggest, nor the sleekest, nor the most mysterious. The Phillips Collection in Washington (1612 21st Street N.W.) is housed primarily in a dowdy old brick mansion that would probably fit into the entrance

hall of the National Gallery. While impressive enough, its collection (mostly modern) is probably less valuable than the paintings stored at any one time in the basement of the Metropolitan.

What makes the Phillips so special is the accessibility of its art. Duncan Phillips, its founder, believed that paintings should be lived with. Most rooms are comfortably furnished with overstuffed sofas, and visitors are encouraged to make use of them. Spend a morning, if you like, reading a novel in the company of Renoir's *Luncheon of the Boating Party,* Cézanne's *Jardin des Lauves,* or a wall of Braques. Or listen, free of charge, to chamber music presented weekly in the elegant former dining hall. If you are so moved, ask questions of the Phillips staff; the reception desk is usually staffed by an art-history student.

THE BEST BACKPACK

No yawns from the urban sophisticates, please. Don't knock it until you've tried it, but don't try it without good equipment. The wrong pack can turn a weekend commune with nature into the heartbreak of sciatica. Backpacks come in a half-dozen styles and over thirty brands, with prices ranging from $15 to $200. Below, a guide through the consumer wilderness.

The best backpack is the one that is most easily forgotten. Strength, convenience, durability, are important. But the bottom line is comfort. Here two factors count: fit and weight-bearing design. Packs usually come in three or four sizes, occasionally with separate shapes for men and women. Mail-order purchasing is chancy, since fit depends on individual body shape and torso length rather than over-

all height. Better to settle for a second-rate brand than risk a second-rate fit.

The basic design is critical because fatigue and muscle strain are minimized only if the weight of the pack rests near your center of gravity. Generally this means that the loaded pack rests high on the shoulders, forcing you to compensate only very slightly by leaning forward. Hip-loaded packs, the latest fashion in full-sized backpacks, distribute weight between shoulders and hips. Traditionalists scorn such newfangled gadgetry, yet anyone carrying forty pounds up a rocky slope or forced to make good time cross-country with a heavy load will offer thanks to the technology god.

Full-Size, Rigid-Frame Packs. For heavy loads, you can't beat the Alpenlite Wraparound-Hipcarry ($88). Its capacity is relatively modest, but the Alpenlite excels in comfort and convenience. Lots of external pockets, including one for maps that can be reached without fuss. Big, jamproof zippers; exceedingly strong frame.

If you take backpacking more casually, the J. C. Penney pack ($35) rates as a best buy. The Penney hip-belt design is as comfortable as the Alpenlite's, and Penney's convenience features are competitive. All you really sacrifice is durability.

Small Loads. At two thirds the capacity and two thirds the price, intermediate-size packs are often a better bet than full-size. They come with either rigid frames or flexible aluminum frames, or they are designed to hold their shape without frames, once loaded. The Kelty Tour Pack ($62) offers superior quality control, a hip belt, and a four-pocket design for maximum access.

As usual, J. C. Penney wins best-buy honors. Penney's Ruck Sack ($17) is a mite flimsy, but otherwise more than adequate.

• THE BEST BALL PARK

Sure, we know the New Orleans Superdome cost more to build than San Clemente, that the Houston Astrodome made Astroturf a household word, that the new Yankee Stadium runs a deficit equal to the GNP of Romania. Maybe the beer does taste better at Busch Memorial Stadium, maybe the fans are more enthusiastic at Boston's Fenway. But none can compare with Wrigley Field in Chicago.

Why love Wrigley? Let us count the ways. In an age of polyvinyl grass and instant-replay scoreboards, the home of the Cubs remains defiantly—no, that's too strong—determinedly old-fashioned. Wrigley's turf is real, its scoreboard is touched by human hands. Ivy, rather than advertising, covers the outfield wall. Only 37,000 Chicagoans, hardly enough to fill the box seats at Dodger Stadium, can sit down at one time. Most striking of all, Wrigley, unlike every other major-league ball park, has no lights for night games. This makes Wrigley the last hitters' park in the major leagues, the last diamond on which power hitters compete equally with fastball pitchers, allowing fans to stay awake without No Doz.

There's only one reason this well-groomed sixty-two-year-old dinosaur is permitted to survive: the Wrigley family. Wrigleys make money selling Spearmint gum; they spend it running a baseball team. In keeping with this unbusiness-like view of sport, the family tries hard to be a good neighbor. Concessionaires, barred from exploiting their monopoly, charge the lowest prices possible. Seats are wide enough to accommodate the overfed, thanks to a decades-old remodeling that *reduced* Wrigley's capacity by 8,000.

Since fans can't always make it to the park, the Cubs' management allows virtually all home games to be televised.

Noblesse oblige hasn't produced a winner—the Cubbies last owned a pennant in 1945—but it has generated loyalty. While the White Sox battle for the first division on a regular basis, they rarely win the attendance wars with their Northside rivals. In 1975, when the two teams had almost identical records, the Cubs outdrew the Sox by a quarter million. Gum-chewers all, we expect.

• THE BEST BEER

No subject is better suited to smoke out the reverse snob. People who can't tell a Pucci from a Gucci or a Pantera from a Porsche (and proud of it . . .) are happy to pass an evening debating the relative merits of Coors and Olympia. We can tell the difference between a Pucci and a Gucci but are still delighted to offer the last word on this difficult and important topic.

First principles first. Few drinkers like good beer, and the ranks of the minority who do are apparently dwindling. Each year, in response to pressure from consumers, brewers make their beers lighter, fizzier, and more tasteless. In the vanguard is Miller's. Already the successful marketer of one of the least pungent beers in America (High Life), Miller's created an instant cult with Lite, the beer that tastes and looks like Canadian whiskey cut with club soda. Schlitz counterattacked with Light, and other breweries are expected to respond with their own versions, if they can think of another way to spell it. If you believe that the best beer is the one with the fewest calories, or the one that exits the corpus quickest, leaving least evidence of its passage, skip this entry.

Ale vs. Lager vs. Pilsner. Once upon a time these terms had clear meanings. Now it depends upon where you're drinking and what the brewer thinks will sell. Lager, from the German word for "storage," appears randomly, or whenever the ad copywriter lacks imagination.

All beer is made roughly the same way. Ground barley and other grains are simmered with water to break down their starch content into fermentable compounds. This cooked goop is flavored with hops to taste, and then filtered to remove unwanted debris. Next, yeast is added. The little plants feed on the dissolved malt sugars, spewing alcohol

and carbon dioxide as they grow. When the sugars are used up, the beer is pumped off to cold storage, where it ferments a bit more and is clarified.

In Britain, ale is just another word for beer, more often than not attached to beers with a fair share of alcohol. Here at home, though, ale means beer fermented with a special yeast that rises to the top of the brewer's vat. The result is a distinctive, slightly sour taste formerly quite popular in New England. Real ale is now out of fashion everywhere and hard to get (try Ballantine India Pale); the closest alternative in good supply is malt liquor.

Pilsner was once exclusively the name of the beer made in Pilsen, Czechoslovakia. It's still made there, but the style has been copied by hundreds of breweries around the world, most notably in the United States. Good pilsners are pale golden, a touch bitter from a liberal dose of hops, and quite fizzy. The delicate taste, low alcohol content, and fine bubbles make pilsners extremely popular, but expensive to produce. They take time and the best ingredients, both of which are in short supply around Milwaukee and St. Louis. For a taste of the real thing, try Pilsner Urquell at a restaurant or from a high-volume dealer who hasn't kept it around too long. Mexican Carta Blanca is another lovely pilsner on the Czech model.

Cans vs. Bottles vs. Draft. Even after the brewing and aging process is complete, beer remains alive with microorganisms. To keep it from spoiling, the stuff must either be pasteurized—heated rapidly for a few minutes to kill bacteria—or kept cold. Draft beer generally tastes better than the store-bought variety because it is shipped fresh, unpasteurized, in chilled barrels.

A few enterprising breweries do, however, make an effort to sell unpasteurized "draft" beer in bottles or cans for drinking at home. The easy way is to make the beer under sterile conditions and then work extra hard to filter out everything still swimming before packaging. Trouble is, this superfiltering also removes part of the flavoring, leaving very thin beer indeed. To our knowledge, only one brewer, Coors, does it the hard way, literally bottling draft beer and keeping it fresh by refrigerating it from factory to super-market. Coors has a very short life and will spoil completely in a few days if left out of the cold. Yet, for all the trouble and expense, we wish Coors tasted better, instead of just different. Unfortunately there is more to good beer than freshness.

If you don't live in the West where Coors is king, the can vs. bottle controversy may be of more interest. By legend, metal cans impart nasty flavors of their own to beer. But this is strictly glass-container-manufacturer propaganda; the metal is coated with lacquer, making it as anonymous as glass. Don't blame the brewer if you taste paint while slurping beer straight from the can. Bottles, in fact, may be slightly inferior to cans since they allow light in.

No matter what the container, beer deteriorates on the shelf at room temperature. Avoid that lone bottle of Beck's your corner grocery has had in the window display for six months, and drink what you do buy within a few weeks.

Foreign vs. Domestic. Now that the preliminaries are over, we can get down to the nitty-gritty. Is it really worth an extra two dollars a six-pack to drink beer made in Japan or Israel or Germany? The answer is yes, if they are bought fresh. No matter what variety of beer you prefer, there is a foreign brew that is better.

The reasons aren't complicated. American breweries are viciously competitive and generally not very profitable. The big guns—Anheuser-Busch, Schlitz, Pabst, Coors, Miller—

are busy driving small breweries to ruin. What counts are advertising, volume, and cost-accounting; premium ingredients and time just don't pay their way.

The cornerstone to good beer is barley malt. Other starches work, a little for flavor or color, a lot to save money. The average American beer is stretched 60 to 70 percent with the cheapest substitutes, corn and malt syrup, while foreign beers more typically run only 20 to 30 percent non-barley. And that fraction is usually rice. The best hops come from Czechoslovakia. Most American beers use only a dash of these imported hops, and a six-pack of Old Steubenville or Quadruple XXXX on sale at $1.19 may contain no European hops at all.

Time is dollars, so don't expect a cost-conscious brewer to imitate Pilsner Urquell, which cold-stores its young beer in cellars for six months. Most American beer is artificially carbonated like 7-Up. This relieves the producer of a lengthy aging period and secondary fermentation, but yields beer with large, short-lived bubbles.

Among the giant brewers, Anheuser-Busch does lean against the wind, refusing to carbonate Budweiser or Michelob and using rice rather than corn as a malt substitute. As in the case of Coors, however, the extra care and expense don't translate into top-notch beer. Some claim this mediocrity is intentional. Americans are hooked on pilsners—they like their beer pale, bubbly, and with little taste of malt. But serve beer ice-cold, as most Americans prefer, and the delicate taste of even the best pilsner disappears. So premium American beers merely aim to look pretty and go down easy.

By contrast, good foreign beers are legion. Europeans in particular are willing to pay for the best and drink it at a temperature (about fifty degrees) that allows the difference to show through. Taste Kronenbourg (France), Kirin

(Japan), Carlsberg (Denmark), and Whitbread's Pale Ale (England), as well as the aforementioned Pilsner Urquell and Carta Blanca. Then try our own favorite: Würzburger, from Germany.

• **THE BEST BET**

If gambling is folly, the population of fools is surely growing. Estimates of how much is bet annually in the United States vary widely (depending on the motives of the estimator), but $300 to $500 billion probably isn't far wrong. Perhaps 10 percent of that total adheres to the hands of bookies, casinos, police, and so on, which puts gambling as a national service industry right up there with dog food, airlines, and advertising, and not far from hospital care.

Since the $30 to $50 billion has to come from someone's pocket, it's a cinch the average gambler is a loser. No one knows how many losers there are for every winner, but probably most winners are professionals who stick to games of skill (i.e., poker and backgammon). With simple (or complicated) games of chance, the long haul is always straight down.

Either way, it's nice to know the odds. For every $100 risked, the average return ranges:

Illegal Sports Betting	$ $
BASEBALL	88.89–99.12
BASKETBALL	91.67–95.45
HOCKEY	91.67–95.45
FOOTBALL	91.67–95.45
BOXING	90.00–95.45
HORSE RACING	80.00–90.00

23

Legal Horse Racing

U.S. TRACKS	79–88
NEW YORK CITY OFF-TRACK	75–79
PUERTO RICO OFF-TRACK	56–57
FRANCE OFF-TRACK	84–86

Illegal Lotteries

IRISH SWEEPSTAKES	30–40
NUMBERS (POLICY BETTING)	50–65
PUNCHBOARDS	30–50

Legal State Lotteries   30–50

Casino Games of Chance

KENO	75–80
SLOT MACHINES	60–95
ROULETTE—MONTE CARLO	97.30–98.90
ROULETTE—LAS VEGAS	92.10–94.80
CRAPS	78.00–99.40
BACCARAT	85.00–98.90

Casino Games of Skill

BLACKJACK	94–100+

Notice that illegal sports bookies pay about as well, or even a bit better, than racetracks. Baseball, hockey, basketball, and football are particularly good buys. Figuring the exact odds on these games is tricky, but two points are easy to remember: betting on the favored team is generally cheaper than betting against; the very best odds are obtained only on large bets.

Not every book will quote the same odds on every game, since each entrepreneur offers odds intended to balance his/her risk. Hence, in theory, it might be possible to bet both sides (with separate bookies) and win money no matter how the game turns out. Gamblers spend lifetimes looking for action like this, but thanks to the telephone they almost never find it.

Racing bookies simply pay off at track odds with the exception of long shots; if the parimutuel odds on the horse you like are longer than 25 to 1, it may be smart to obey the law and go to the track.

New York OTB is a special rip-off as the payoff percentages clearly show. Actually, it's even worse: OTB reports big winners to the IRS. The Puerto Rican OTB system, confined to combination betting, is really meant to compete with the local numbers game. Tickets cost less than 50 cents and, on rare occasions, winners have received as much as $100,000.

Regular lotteries, legal and illegal, remain about the worst bets imaginable. The states that have gone into the business for themselves are all very greedy ("crime shouldn't pay"), returning less than 50 cents of every dollar wagered. True odds on some of the open-ended million-dollar lotteries are very difficult to calculate in advance, since the prize money is fixed while the number of tickets sold can vary. The Irish Sweepstakes, by the way, are perfectly legal in Ireland, but ticket sales in the United States are illegal. This, however, does not stop the IRS from taxing winners.

Craps is far and away the biggest moneymaker for Nevada's casinos, yet, paradoxically, it remains the game of chance with the most favorable odds. Only smart bettors get those odds: 26 of the 36 possible bets in craps compare unfavorably with the 5–8 percent average house take on roulette. Remember, too, that the action is so fast in craps that a minimal 1–2 percent house edge is often enough to wipe out the smartest bettor in short order.

Slot machines and keno (a streamlined form of bingo) are strictly for suckers: tourists with a few hundred dollars to blow, compulsive gamblers who take their masochism very seriously. Interestingly, attempts to replace the standard one-arm bandit with button-operated electronic marvels have been met with stubborn resistance by the clientele. Where are you when we need you, Sigmund?

American casinos offer only one true game of skill— poker. Poker parlors in Nevada and California make money by charging a flat fee for the use of their facilities. Hence the house percentage depends upon the speed and stakes of the players. Blackjack also contains elements of skill. By following a very simple strategy, it's possible to cut the odds favoring the dealer down to about 6 percent. Much more difficult systems, pioneered by Arizona math professor Edward Thorp, can actually turn the odds a few percentage points in favor of the player, but there's a catch (or two). First, you must have a good memory, since winning depends upon keeping track of the cards as they are dealt. Second, the dealer can foil the system by using several decks at a time or by shuffling before the end of the deck, or by kicking you out of the casino.

• THE BEST BUTTER

As you know too well, butter is death. Ounce for ounce it is the highest of high-calorie foods (3,200 calories to the pound); healthy coronary arteries clog up merely at the sight of a cholesterol-laden pat. You also know that butter, alas, is the golden fulcrum of taste, the active ingredient in almost every delicious food from chocolate frosting to sauce béarnaise. What to do? Avoid the stuff if possible, but when flesh is weak, spread only the best.

The United States Department of Agriculture grades serve as a pretty good start. Butter ratings run from AA to A to B to ungraded. Any AA brand will proudly announce that fact on the carton. However, since ratings are voluntary, packages containing lesser grades are not likely to be so informative.

USDA AA butter meets a high standard on texture and freedom from extraneous flavor, but the rating allows quite a range of color and taste. Color usually depends upon how much food dye is added, since the natural color of butter varies from white to a very pale yellow. Most of us think butter should be canary yellow, so producers oblige. But don't be put off by the real thing.

Assuming AA butter is sold fresh, taste variations largely depend upon salt content and what the cows ate. Very serious fat consumers generally prefer their butter sweet or with only a hint of salt, since salt tends to cover subtle flavors. If you do buy sweet butter, remember that it will show faint signs of rancidity long before the salted type.

Experts insist that East Coast cows eat better than their Midwest counterparts, producing a richer-tasting spread. Whether true or not, this information isn't likely to do you much good if you purchase national brand names or supermarket private labels. The big butter distributors buy supplies wherever it is convenient and cheap.

The best butter we know in the United States comes from the few local creameries that still package under their own names; check gourmet food stores and expensive independent groceries for these unfamiliar labels. Two very superior imported brands (selling for roughly twice the price of

Land O Lakes), the French Beurre d'Isigny and Danish Lurpak, can sometimes be found in the same specialty stores. Both are lightly salted but in other respects quite different. Lurpak, dense and elastic even at room temperature, has an extremely mild flavor. Beurre d'Isigny has a more assertive taste of cream.

C
THE BEST CAR STEREO

Sure it's decadent, tooling down the interstate, AC on max and tape deck on Wings. But don't knock it until you've tried it.

With few exceptions, stereo units hung on new cars by the manufacturers are overpriced junk, stuff you'd buy for $24.95 at Sears so your six-year-old could listen to nursery rhymes. Maybe this is just to match the cars themselves— no need to confuse the customers with quality. More likely, it follows from a misunderstanding; competition from engine and road noise do not render the ear incapable of distinguishing good fidelity from bad. Herewith, three options, depending upon whether you're (a) interested, (b) rich, or (c) out of your gourd.

Honest Music. Apart from general mediocrity, the biggest problem with standard-equipment stereos is the speaker system. Typically, car speakers do a C+ job on bass and flunk the high notes completely. So the cheapest possible improvement is to substitute a pair of decent speakers capable of accurate sound reproduction across the mid-range; we suggest rear-deck-mounted Jensen C9740's ($74 a pair). Other speakers at much lower prices produce equivalent sound, but the Jensens make exceptionally small power demands on anemic car stereo amplifiers.

The next step up is an add-on AM/FM receiver and/or a cassette player. Craig's Model 1902 AM/FM radio ($120) has a clean-sounding amp, and the tuner section is satisfactorily sensitive. Another possibility: the Panasonic CR-714 EU ($120). We opt for cassettes over the more popular eight-track tapes because eight-track fidelity is inferior. A little deck like the Lafayette RK 300 ($90) will do a fine job on prerecorded tapes and won't shame cassette recordings made with good-quality components.

Mid-Size. If you really care about high fidelity and don't mind paying for it, take a giant step up to the ADS 2002 amp/speaker combo ($400 a pair), designed to match the Nakamichi Model 250 or 350 cassette player ($275). Rear-deck-mounted ADS speakers take care of the

power problem with external booster amps, delivering up to 40 watts where it counts. In spite of their compact dimensions (7 × 4 × 4 inches), ADS speakers are terrific, easily a match for your average $150 acoustic suspension home speakers. Like expensive component cassette decks, the Nakamichi has equalization switches to play ferric or chrome tapes, and a built-in Dolby noise-reduction system. Dolby makes a big difference because high-frequency tape hiss stands out over lower-frequency automobile background noises.

The most sensitive AM/FM car radio is the gadget-filled Becker Grand Prix ($600). At that price, it should be special. The Grand Prix searches out signals automatically and lets you tune in short-wave broadcasts, too. Regrettably (or fortunately—it's a question of taste) the Becker has a special mellow sound unique to expensive European radios. If you don't like your music filtered through Valium, consider the Motorola FM485AX ($120), a good all-round radio.

Ne Plus Ultra. The core of the ultimate car stereo is a modular monster called the Blaupunkt Berlin ($1,015). It does everything but protect your vehicle from surface-to-air missiles, combining an AM/FM tuner, a cassette player that can also take dictation or record telephone conversations, and a powerful amplifier. The cassette goes under the dash, while the guts of the tuner and amplifier fit in a box that stows in the truck. Controls for the radio and tape machine are on the end of a flexible gooseneck stalk that can be positioned between front bucket seats, or anywhere else you fancy. Need we add that the radio includes a scanning device for finding stations and an electronic memory lest you misplace one.

Nothing beats those ADS speakers. Here buy Model

2001 ($500) units designed to function without aid from the Nakamichi cassette deck.

• THE BEST CAVIAR

Times are tough all over, but you wouldn't guess it by the sales of caviar. From Palm Springs to Palm Beach, folks are plunking down their nickels in record quantity to savor the fresh raw eggs of the Caspian Sea sturgeon. About 15,000 pounds will be consumed in 1976, at prices ranging from $70 to $125 a pound.

If you think rich people are out of their minds paying this much for fish eggs, it's probably because you have never tried the real thing. Most caviar (all the caviar found on the grocery shelf) is pasteurized and vacuum-packed. Such processed caviar is cheap—well, relatively cheap—and has the advantage of remaining edible for years, like most canned goods. Unfortunately, it tastes like pleasantly salty fish paste. A nice change from smoked oysters or hearts of palm on the hors d'oeuvre tray, perhaps, but hardly worth its weight in macadamia nuts.

The best caviar is packed uncooked and remains fresh under refrigeration for only two or three weeks. The Russian variety has a certain cachet; however, it's identical to Iranian caviar sold at slightly lower prices. In fact, some importers suspect that Russian caviar is actually repackaged Iranian. Pollution on the Russian side of the Caspian has reduced the sturgeon population so much that the USSR has begun to import supplies from the Shah.

Whether Iranian or Russian, market value is determined by the size of the caviar grain, its color, and its saltiness. The very best is light gray beluga (large-grain) malassol—

31

malassol meaning packed with very little salt as a preservative. Fresh beluga bears no resemblance to pasteurized. The taste and aroma bring to mind sea spray on a cool day, or perhaps just the shameless security of feeling rich. Smaller-grained sevruga malassol is slightly less perfect, but often a bargain at about two thirds the price of beluga. For the hopelessly corrupt who cannot afford to feed their habits, there's fresh pressed caviar (*payasnaya*) at about $2 per ounce. Pressed caviar takes getting used to; it comes in unaesthetic sticky, chewy blocks, but tastes much like beluga.

Caviar is traditionally garnished with chopped egg, onion, and sour cream and served with iced vodka or dry champagne. If the caviar is good, we believe extra fixings just get in the way: all that's really needed is a few drops of lemon juice and a spoon. Should you choose the champagne route, splurge on a bottle of Taittinger Blanc de Blanc or Louis Roederer Cristal. Champagnes made from the darker Pinot Noir grape, even very great ones, dominate the flavor of extremely delicate food. Among domestic champagnes, the most suitable are Schramsberg Blanc de Blanc and Gold Seal Natural.

Of course, all this good advice is worthless unless caviar is available. That's no problem in big cities, but elsewhere the risk of paying a fortune for over-the-hill beluga is high. Insist on a look and a sniff before you buy. Fresh caviar should be shiny and unwrinkled, with no sign of milky liquid between grains. If the local supply doesn't make the grade, there's still a way. One extremely reliable, high-volume New York purveyor, Caviarteria, Inc. (870 Madison Avenue) will ship air-freight, guaranteed fresh arrival anywhere in the United States, at the going store price (about $75 for 14 ounces) plus $5 handling.

• THE BEST CHOCOLATE CHIP COOKIE

The best CCC is a subject too important to trust to any individual, even the author. Hence we assembled an impartial panel of four cookie experts to evaluate twenty-two brands, including the major supermarket contenders from Nabisco, Keebler, Quaker Oats, and Sunshine. All brands were purchased off the shelf in the New York City area; prices listed below were competitive, but none reflect occasional specials.

Since it's hardly fair to compare 79-cents-a-pound A&P cookies with bakery brands selling for three times as much, elite CCC's were rated separately. A third category, chippers that contain unusual flavors, such as peanut butter or coconut, was also included. Cookies were judged on four criteria: texture, flavor, chip density, and over-all impression. The panel was given no direction as to what constituted the ideal cookie, since there are many conflicting schools of thought on this matter. Where panelists' views diverged sharply, we note the disagreement. Chip density is what it sounds like: the quantity of chocolate per bite. More chocolate does not necessarily a better cookie make; use the information with caution. Brands are listed within each category in descending order of quality.

On the whole, the panelists were surprised by the low quality of mass-market brands. CCC's rated Fair or Poor are generally very sweet and very boring, their manufacturers aiming at tastebuds under the age of ten. Two of the most serious offenders, Chip-A-Roos and Chips Ahoy!, appeal directly to the "Captain Kangaroo" set with cartoon stories on the package to tie in with TV advertising.

The best chocolate chip cookie, by consensus, is Mrs. A's Choco-Crunch. In one sense this is surprising, since Mrs. A's owes so little to the classic Toll House style. One might note, however, that it is one of only two cookies tested made with butter instead of vegetable shortening.

Much has been written about The Famous Amos CCC and its rival, The Famous. Amos got his start in 1975, vending chippers to the stars in Hollywood. The Famous appeared from nowhere a year later with a cookie in a similar brown bag and almost identical ingredients. Who is imitating whom we can't say, but our panelists strongly preferred the West Coast version. The Famous Amos are smaller, thinner, and firmer, with a more pleasing chocolate/pecan balance. Readers who prefer a large meaty CCC might do well to buy The Famous in the nutless variant.

The other well-known cookie on the list, Pepperidge Farm, is not in the same league with the other elite brands. Save for its pleasing crispness, the panelists would have rated it on a par with losers like Chips Ahoy! and Jane Parker.

Among supermarket brands, Keebler cookies scored uniformly high. Our panelists liked the dense, almost greasy, Pecan Sandie-ish style of the check-rated C.C. Biggs, and were equally impressed by Keebler Coconut Chocolate Drops and Rich'N Chips. Natural-food freaks will find little comfort in these taste ratings: all three Keeblers contain chemical emulsifiers (sorbitan monostearate, polysorbate 60), while the high-ranking Burry's Best are stabilized with BHA and propyl gallate. Only Mrs. Carver's, however, can boast the likes of sodium stearoyl-2-lactylate, BHA, *and* BHT.

	$/LB.	TEXTURE	FLAVOR	CHIP DENSITY	GESTALT

ELITE

MRS. A'S CHOCO-CRUNCH	2.37	VG	E	VG	E

(Mrs. Anderson's Kitchens, Monroe, Conn.)
Crunchy, buttery, distinct brown-sugar taste

THE FAMOUS AMOS	3.00	VG	VG	E	E

(The Famous Amos, Hollywood)
Small flat cookies, very large chips, crispy, clean butter/sugar taste

THE FAMOUS	3.00	G	VG	E	VG

(The Famous CCC, Roslyn, N.Y.)
Traditional style, too many nuts obscure chocolate

	$/LB.	TEXTURE	FLAVOR	CHIP DENSITY	GESTALT

MRS. CARVER'S 2.95 VG VG VG VG
(Carver Foods, Houston)
Butter flavor; solid, almost dense, not chewy or crisp

SUSAN'S GIANT 2.80 F G E G
(Barbara's Bakery, San Francisco)
Rich in walnuts and chips, sub-par mealy texture, 100 percent whole wheat flour

PEPPERIDGE FARM 2.02 VG F F G
(Norwalk, Conn.)
Bland, underchipped, overrated; not really a premium cookie

COMBINATIONS

**COCONUT CHOCO-
LATE DROPS** 1.11 VG VG VG VG
(Keebler)
Pleasantly greasy, nicely balanced, lots of coconut

RICH'N CHIPS 1.11 VG G F VG
(Keebler)
Unusual peanut-butter flavor good complement to chips

CHOC-CO CHIPS 1.11 F F F F
(Nabisco)
Suffers badly by comparison with Keebler; anemic

MASS MARKET

C. C. BIGGS 1.09 VG VG VG VG
(Keebler)
Familiar greasy Keebler feel, fine basic cookie

BURRY'S BEST 1.58 VG VG E VG
(Burry/Quaker Oats)
Same style as Pepperidge Farm, but better flavor and more chips

**FFV CHOCOLATE
DROP** 1.18 VG VG F VG
(FFV)
Surprising light texture, vanilla-dominated flavor

	$/LB.	TEXTURE	FLAVOR	CHIP DENSITY	GESTALT

ARCHWAY CHIP-
CHIP   1.29   VG   F   VG   G
(Archway)
Chewy, full of chips, but bland; panelists disagreed on overall score

BURRY, MR. CHIPS   1.17   G   G   G   G
(Burry/Quaker Oats)
Crisp, nicely balanced, clearly a supermarket cookie, but okay

JANE PARKER   .98   G   F   G   F
(A&P)
Distinct artificial vanilla taste, otherwise satisfactory

PETER PAUL
CHOCO CHIP   1.22   G   F   P   F
(Peter Paul, Chicago)
Imitation Keebler texture, quite sweet, chips almost tasteless

CHIPS AHOY!   1.09   VG   F   F   F
(Nabisco)
Very nutty, very sweet; acceptable only if you don't like chocolate

ARCHWAY ICEBOX
CHOCOLATE CHIP   1.00   G   P   F   F
(Archway)
Nice icebox texture, but no flavor; panelists disagreed on overall score

BURRY CHOCO-
LATE CHIP   1.05   F   P   G   F
(Burry/Quaker Oats)
Poor chocolate taste, too sweet, very artificial

CHIP-A-ROOS   .98   F   P   F   F
(Sunshine)
Very sweet, boring; made for kids

MAMA'S   .94   F   P   F   F
(Mama Baking Company, Chicago)
Artificial vanilla taste, extremely bland

FRESH 'N GOOD   .78   F   P   F   P
(United Biscuit)
Inferior in every way; cheap source of calories, though

• THE BEST CLOCK

Accutron tuning-fork watches rarely miss by more than a minute per month, provided they are insulated against temperature extremes. Quartz crystal watches, from the lowliest $15.95 department-store loss leader to the fanciest Pulsar, are tenfold more accurate—figure a minute a year as par. Quartz laboratory clocks cut the numbers yet finer, to something on the order of half a second per annum. Good enough to catch the 5:58 to Brewster, perhaps, but well short of the record.

The best clock is an atomic hydrogen maser oscillator owned by the U.S. Naval Laboratory in Washington. Now, timepieces all work on the same principle, counting the number of times some extremely regular event takes place. In a grandfather clock, it's the swing of a pendulum; in an Accutron, the vibrations of a tuning fork; in a Quartz watch, the natural electronic frequency of a crystal. Atomic clocks count the electronic resonances of atoms excited by radiation. These resonances are so rapid and so uniform that it's possible to slice time very finely: atomic clocks, run with hydrogen, oscillate at almost 1,420,450,751,694 cycles a second. Hydrogen maser clocks aren't quite perfect, you understand. They wander about one second every 300,000 years. To come closer to perfection, the naval lab runs twin hydrogen masers and then averages the result.

If your major concern is not missing the opening credits on "Upstairs, Downstairs," atomic clocks may not be necessary. However, electronic navigation systems like loran would be worthless without super-accurate clocks, as would new collision warning equipment in airplanes and elaborate remote-control communications links for NASA's deep-space probes. The most mind-boggling use of atomic clocks has been to test Einstein's general theory of relativity. As every SF fan knows, the relativity theory predicts that time

"slows down" for objects moving rapidly or subjected to strong gravitational fields. Hence the paradox of the space voyager who returns to earth to find his or her grandchildren long dead. The spaceship would have to move at a good clip to achieve this, however: a jet circling the globe at 500 miles per hour gains less than a millionth of a second on each trip.

In 1971 two physicists precisely measured that gain, carrying four atomic clocks around the world in Boeing 707's. Flying west at about 30,000 feet, the clocks ended up an average of 273 *billionths* of a second out of sync with the master time standard in Washington. Einstein's theory predicted a gain of 275 billionths, give or take a moment.

• THE BEST COFFEE

Judging by the oceans of sour, silt-colored fluid swilled each day, coffee addicts care little for the aesthetics of this miraculous narcotic. But if you wish to opt out of the Maxpax generation, pay close attention.

Beans. Forget instant coffees. A decent instant could be manufactured, but producers greedily overextract the soluble part from the coffee beans. Ground coffee fresh from the can sometimes tastes just fine, but few brands contain premium beans and virtually all are lightly roasted to avoid offending the most nervous palate. Even if you do find a brand that satisfies, chances are your friendly neighborhood conglomerate will vary the blend within a year or two.

Far better, then, to purchase coffee in the bean and grind it fresh to order at home. Roasted beans last a month in the fridge and three to four, tightly sealed, in the freezer. All beans worth grinding are of the arabica species; robustas, grown mostly in Africa, are used for instant or inexpensive canned brands. Among arabicas, a half-dozen varieties stand out. Which is best is truly a matter of taste.

The most famous, and most costly, is unblended Jamaica Blue Mountain at four to five dollars a pound. It excels in aroma and mellowness, the qualities necessary for the perfect American-style cup. Close substitutes, sometimes available in specialty stores, include Hawaiian Kona and Venezuelan Maracaibo. The other legendary beans, Mocha from the tiny Middle Eastern state of Yemen, and Java, from Indonesia, are usually blended with less regal Brazilian varieties. Without adulteration, both make rich, heavily flavored coffees with a noticeably acid finish, the ideal accompaniment for cakes and cream pies. Pure Mocha-Java is a delicious traditional blend of the two rare coffees. Confusingly, "Mocha-Java Blend" need only be a blended coffee containing unspecified amounts of Mocha and Java.

Coffee blends, incidentally, are not necessarily inferior to unblended. The house blend at coffee stores—usually based on Brazilian Santos—is often first rate and a safer choice, potluck, than mysterious mélanges called Kona Blend, Mocha Blend, and so on.

The one great coffee family easily purchased unblended is Colombian. Any true Colombian found in the United States is okay or better. Good stores provide the very best ones, from the Medellin, Manizales, and Armenia regions. These are beans of a balance that produces medium-rich coffee of varying characteristics, depending upon how the beans are roasted.

Roasts. All coffee must be roasted, but the length of

the roasting time has a lot to do with the taste of the cup. At the anemic end of the spectrum are "light city" roasts, pale brown beans made to order for people who wish their daily measure of caffeine to taste as little as possible like coffee. In the middle are "full city" roasts; here the beans come dark brown, but still dull-colored and dry to the touch. Full city roasts are ideal for high-quality filter or drip coffee, rich-tasting but not rich enough to overwhelm subtle differences between varieties of bean.

The darkest roast is called Italian or Espresso; the beans are jet black and shiny from oils forced to the surface during long roasting. Espresso roasts like Medaglia d'Oro mask the complexity of coffee flavor but can provide a satisfying jolt. Slightly less dark Cuban or French-Italian roast lets more of the bean through to the taste bud, but lacks equivalent muscle—an espresso without tears. Two commercial brands available on the East Coast roasted this way are Bustelo and El Pico.

Coffee stores usually sell popular varieties and blends as full city roasts, then offer a few dark roasts without specifying the beans in the blend. If none of these anonymous blends pleases, try another store or ask the manager to sell you unroasted beans and do it yourself.

Brewing. Boil up a pot of freshly ground, five-dollar-a-pound Jamaica Blue Mountain in your GE percolator and it will taste remarkably like day-old Maxwell House. The only advantage to the percolator is convenience, a dubious distinction shared by frozen fish sticks, condensed books, and nylon Christmas trees. Luckily the automatic electric drip maker is making deep inroads in percolator land, and total victory is in sight.

Almost everyone knows how to make a bad cup of

coffee; it's how to make a good cup that starts arguments. In truth, there are two excellent methods and a number of satisfactory variations of these two. Take your pick:

Method No. 1: Filtration. The secret to good coffee is keeping the right amount of coffee in contact for the right amount of time with the right amount of water heated to the right temperature. Follow the directions on a standard Melitta or Chemex pot and you are not likely to miss. The paper filter provides a reliable control on the length of the brewing process and also removes extraneous solids from the finished cup. Automatic electric drip makers work the same way, but not all models distribute hot water evenly over the grounds and some manufacturers mislead on the proper ratio of water to coffee. Two brands that do work well are Norelco and Bunn-O-Matic.

Method No. 2: Espresso. The principal differences between the espresso and filter method are the temperature of the water and the time the coffee and water spend together. A true espresso machine forces a mixture of steam and boiling water through finely ground coffee in just a matter of seconds. The result—assuming good, dark-roast beans have been used—is an extremely assertive brew completely free of the bitter taste of super-strong drip coffee.

The best espresso machine around is the Italian Pavoni. It costs a fortune (around $200 and climbing), but compensates with extreme durability, built-in heating coils, and a bonus attachment to steam milk for cappucino.

• THE BEST COMMENT ON NEW YORK CITY'S FINANCES

In an effort to cut expenditures, the New York State Legislature recently required the city university to impose tuition. Students requesting assistance in paying the new charges were asked to call the university's financial aid office at 999–1234, a number previously assigned to Dial-A-Joke.

• THE BEST CONVERTIBLE

A sneaky entry, you say? The convertible is dead, buried by the Cadillac division of General Motors, which produced its last Eldorado (a.k.a. the Pimpmobile) in 1976. GM made certain you'd remember the funeral, of course, adding red and white stripes and a brass plate to the last 200 "Bicentennial" specials. Inflamed by patriotism, speculators pushed the price of these street yachts to $50,000 quicker than you could purr "rich Corinthian leather."

Actually, the convertible is far from dead. Eleven genuine fabric-top cars (not counting Targa/roll bar compromises) are still imported—seven from England, two each from Germany and Italy. Contrary to Detroit-inspired legend, the convertible is not illegal and not about to become illegal. It's true the feds declared war on soft tops years ago, but the courts ruled that convertible buyers, like cigarette smokers, had the right to risk their lives if they pleased. The Big Three phased out convertibles only because they anticipated losing the legal battle. By the time free enterprise triumphed the die was cast: Ford, Chrysler, and GM decided they preferred the mark-ups on sun roofs.

Some imports are old-fashioned sports cars—fun to drive, if leaky, noisy, and a bit hard on the gluteus. The Triumph (TR6 and Spitfire), MG Midget, and MGB fit this category. (The MG's, though, are only fun to drive during those infrequent intervals when their electrical systems are functioning.) Your more bourgeois Alfa Romeo Spider, Fiat Sport Spyder, and Jensen-Healy, and the positively regal Mercedes Benz 450SL are put together with care, but we don't think they should be compared with traditional convertibles, since they seat only two passengers.

That leaves three soft tops in the competition: the Rolls-Royce Corniche, VW Beetle, and Jensen Interceptor. Now, justifiably, the Corniche has its fans. The hides of seven blemish-free cows cover the seats, a walnut forest covers everything else. At sixty miles per hour the loudest sounds are the bubbles from the Taittinger Blanc de Blancs. However, for $70,000 plus, we think a convertible should be more than a limousine with the roof sawed off. The Corniche is overweight and undersuspended, cornering no better than an LTD or Cordoba.

About as far from Corniche as you can go, there's the world's most popular convertible, the Beetle. It hasn't

changed much in the last three decades, putting on a few pounds to meet federal bumper specs, adopting fuel injection to clean up an engine first conceived to power Wehrmacht jeeps. Some love the no-nonsense plastic upholstery and skittish, super-quick, cornering. We don't, but then we're poor sports.

Our favorite, the Jensen Interceptor, is almost as old in design as the Beetle. Here, though, it's a matter of preserving class. Jensen has never caught on with the Mercedes/Jaguar/Citroën crowd, and the manufacturers are always

threatening to cut their losses. This would be a pity, since the Interceptor deserves to be ranked with the great GT's. Outside, the car comes on long and lean. Inside, it's all leather and toggle switches, more Beverly Hills than Mayfair. The Jensen people assume that anyone who can afford an Interceptor ($25,000) can afford to waste gas. Hence the 260-horse cast-iron Chrysler V-8 under the hood, power to spare at 100 mph. The big surprise, though, is the way the Interceptor makes its peace with the road. Real sports-car manners just wouldn't do. But the Interceptor's power-assisted steering responds well, even when you push. If Jaguar made a convertible, this is how it would feel.

• THE BEST CUBAN RESTAURANT IN MIAMI

Even if you've done your duty on line at Joe's Stone Crab, admired the Tiffany glass over steaks at the Forge, and sampled the deli at Wolfie Cohen's Rascal House, Miami still has one surprise left. Risk a voyage to the mainland—more specifically, to the strip of Eighth Street in old Miami known as Little Havana—for a meal at Centro Vasco.

Actually, Miami has a number of first-rate Cuban restaurants: the modest Minerva and much more ambitious Viscaya come to mind. But our favorite is the Centro Vasco, whose blinking lights and pink dolphin fountain compete for attention with the car dealers, funeral parlors, and furniture showrooms along the Tamiami Trail. Inside, the Centro Vasco looks like every Mexican/Spanish/Basque restaurant: bullfight and jai alai posters on stucco walls, a great dark-wood bar, wrought-iron wagonwheel chandeliers.

Owner Juanito Saizarbitoria, brought the restaurant to

Miami from Cuba in 1962. The menu reflects Saizerbitoria's Basque birthplace (he fought on the losing side in the Spanish Civil War), but some of the nicest dishes are strictly Caribbean. Start with Frijoles Negros (black beans on rice loaded with chopped onion) or Sopa de Porrusalda, a Basque potato soup. Filet Madrilène (breaded filet mignon stuffed with sausage and cheese) is the most acclaimed main course, though we prefer the Filete de Cerdo, broiled pork with rice and beans and fried bananas. The *pargo* (red snapper) dishes are also worth trying.

Centro Vasco has a decent selection of Spanish wines; a red Rioja Reserva and a very young white bottled by Bodegas F. Paternina are notable. We recommend drinking good imported beer instead, unless you opt for one of the seafood entries. Pass up the desserts if you like ice cream: King Cream Helados, several blocks down Eighth Street, serves magnificent fresh-fruit ice creams (coconut, mango, pineapple, and so on), an amazing Cuban invention.

• **THE BEST CURE FOR AN ACHING BACK**

Fashions change, even in disease. Digestive problems used to top the complaint list, with ulcers the common cause. But in the last decade or so, the sore-tummy epidemic has receded and backache has come into its own. Back pain is a symptom of dozens of maladies—kidney disease, cancer, bone infections, rheumatoid arthritis, arteriosclerosis—and self-diagnosis can be a dangerous game. The vast majority (85 percent) of sufferers, though, are simply victims of tension, obesity, poor posture, or underexercise.

The culprit is evolution. Humans may have picked up a few Darwinian points by learning to stand, and run, on two legs, but the back was never really properly designed for the job. Not merely must the vertebrae and supporting muscles, cartilage, and so forth, protect the spine, they must accommodate complex motion and endure awesome stress. For people conditioned by chopping wood and plowing fields from childhood to old age, the back often makes it through a lifetime unscathed. But for those of us who specialize in pushing pencils and shifting from park to drive, backs are the weakest link. Occasionally they collapse with a bang, done in by weekend tennis; more frequently they rebel after a thousand minor insults.

Pain, particularly in the lower back, that never seems severe enough to take seriously, yet never goes away for very long, is the standard warning of big trouble to come. If you ignore it and are unlucky, you'll end up with a ruptured disk or arthritis. Herewith a checklist of virtuous activities that should make the pain go away, as well as improve the odds your back will outlast your heart and other useful organs.

Exercise, with care. Exercise is *the* key to beating the odds. Yet most strenuous exercises—almost all that are fun—are more likely to hurt than help. The very best back exercise (other than specific stomach-, leg-, and back-strengthening calisthenics) is swimming; crawl or side-stroke preferred. Swimming comes close to perfection because, under water, gravity and accompanying lower-back stress are neutralized. Jogging on turf or cinders in good track shoes isn't bad, either. Competition sports like tennis, handball, and squash are risky unless you are in excellent condition, while contact sports like football and basketball court disaster.

Stand straight. Believe it or not, all that stuff they fed you in seventh grade about good posture was true. Improper distribution of weight speeds the natural aging process, with increased risk of osteoarthritis, chronic muscle spasm, and disk injury. While your gym teacher was right about the problem, he/she was wrong about the solution. "Stomach in, shoulders back, chest out" doesn't work. Instead, try elevating your head with your chin tucked in, simultaneously tightening your buttocks. Also, avoid standing for long periods with your feet side by side; this puts excessive stress on the lower back. If you must stand, put one foot up on a stool (or bar rail), alternating feet every few minutes.

Sit straight. Almost every comfortable chair is a no-no. A good chair provides support in the small of the back and allows you to lean forward rather than forcing you backward. Car seats, of course, rarely meet these requirements, which is why long-distance driving is verboten for back sufferers. Bucket seats are generally worse than benches, squooshy seats worse than firm. To minimize strain on the lumbar area, sit close enough to the pedals so that your knees are bent.

Sleep straight. As with sitting, luxury is sin. Soft mattresses are bad; firm ones are good—the harder the better. If you can stand the idea, sleep on the floor. An unyielding surface distributes weight where it belongs. Lie on your side with one leg drawn up, or sleep on your back. Most important, avoid sleeping on your stomach: it exaggerates the natural tendency toward swayback.

Think straight. Tension often translates into lower-back pain or less predictable back muscle spasms. Twenty or thirty years of taking your frustrations out in the lumbar muscles can lead to a whole textbook full of depressing degenerative conditions. This warning is only for the record, of course. Telling chronic worriers about the dangers of worrying only gives them something else to worry about.

THE BEST DOMINO

M. Gérard Gasson, an elderly schoolteacher, avoided injury when his 1936 Citroën sedan stalled on a railroad crossing one night in March '76. Unfortunately, the car was destroyed by a speeding freight train.

More unfortunate still, the collision derailed an $800,000 locomotive, which smashed into the supports of a railroad bridge over the busy Marne-Rhine canal, toppling the steel structure and ripping up an additional hundred yards of track. The locomotive and twenty-five freight cars (worth an average $75,000 each) joined the bridge in the drink shortly thereafter, blocking barge traffic for ten days. Service on the rail bridge was restored after a nine-day delay, much to the relief of the French National Railways, which was forced to make a 150-mile detour around the accident site until repairs were completed.

M. Gasson's insurance company has accepted liability for business losses to both the owners of some forty barges trapped by the wreckage and buyers of the trainload of beer and canned soup; local fishing cooperatives, which lost several hundred pounds of breams, ruffs, and gudgeons when the canal was contaminated by beer and soup, may be forced to litigate. With or without the dead fish, total insurance claims are expected to exceed $5 million. M. Gasson will bear part of the burden, though: his annual premium has been raised from $33 to $38.

 ## THE BEST EFFORT AT JUDICIAL REFORM

Mayor Jimmy Walker of New York once found himself hard pressed to explain why he had placed a City Hall crony on the bench of the children's court. "The appointment of Judge Hylan," explained Walker, "means that children can now be tried by their peer."

· THE BEST ENCYCLOPEDIA

Encyclopedias are like Italian sports cars: nearly everyone who owns one is sorry but is afraid to admit it. Would you confess to opening your door to a perfect stranger, listening to a ridiculous story about how the publisher is giving away twenty-eight-volume review sets to discerning customers, and then plunking down $449 for ten yearbooks and a genuine walnut-colored bookcase? A sports car at least looks pretty parked in the driveway.

If an inner compulsion propels you toward one of the

$449 behemoths, or if you have something saner in mind, read on:

Knowledge by the Ton. The new Encyclopaedia Britannica, Britannica 3 for short, is the longest (43 million words), most authoritative general encyclopedia ever published. And if that's not enough to send you scurrying for your Master Charge, there's a gimmick, too. Britannica 3 is subdivided into a one-volume Propaedia, or Outline of Knowledge, a ten-volume Micropaedia for quick reference, and a nineteen-volume Macropaedia, chock full of long review articles. The Propaedia is almost worthless unless you happen to be a Martian who likes to learn from scratch. But the Macro/Micro arrangement comes off slightly less awkwardly than the conventional index-plus-cross-reference system used in earlier editions. Britannica prose can be a bore—it's been downhill ever since the famous eleventh edition (1911). A bigger problem is the difficulty of the subject matter; Britannica's editors expect much from their readers, occasionally far more than bright high-school students can muster.

Only two other encyclopedias in this category, Collier's and the Encyclopedia Americana, are worth mentioning. Forget the Americana: it's not bad, but ranks as an inferior version of the Britannica. Collier's may tempt, if you want to save some money (expect to pay around $450 versus $700 for the Britannica) and prefer cleaner, streamlined entries. Collier's, incidentally, is as up-to-date as Britannica and should remain so, since it is revised a couple of times each year.

One last possibility: Funk and Wagnalls. At 9 million words, F and W can hardly compete with the biggies. But, then, the biggies cost a lot more than $70. It looks like an encyclopedia (all twenty-seven volumes' worth), smells like an encyclopedia, and is kept reasonably complete and up-to-date. Funk and Wagnalls never peddles door-to-door. You must buy it, a volume per week, at the supermarket. Once the retailer's promotion cycle is over, the publisher allows slackers to fill in the missing volumes by mail order.

One-volume Encyclopedias. Purists object to encyclopedias between a single set of covers. They are superficial by necessity, take up too little room on the shelf, and are guaranteed to rend flesh when dropped. We think at least one of them—the New Columbia—is more useful than all but the best adult giants.

The current (fourth) edition was published in 1975, twelve years after its predecessor; edition four is shorter (by a million words), but typographically easier on the eye than number three. The preface sports a remarkable list of "academic consultants" from Columbia and elsewhere, though it's hard to gauge their influence since the articles are unsigned. NCE no longer wastes space listing every town in America with a population over 1,000; the quaint tradition of maintaining an entry for every proper name in the King James version of the Bible has, however, been retained. The writing style is crisp, if not compelling. Columbia University Press doesn't like to advertise the date of the next revision, since it might get stuck with a warehouse full of the old one. But only the science entries should date rapidly. The regular bookstore price ($80) isn't out of line. Shop around: the NCE is a popular loss leader, selling in some stores for as little as $50.

For less (an astonishing $20) there's the 3-million-word Larousse International Encyclopedia and Dictionary. The Larousse shouldn't be compared with the Columbia: it contains no bibliography, skimps a bit on American entries, ignores lots of important topics, and eschews controversy.

Still, the Larousse is good enough to tell you when Benjamin Franklin died or which countries border Chad.

Children's Encyclopedias. If the aforementioned encyclopedia peddler doesn't stick you with a "free" review edition, chances are he/she will try the guilt approach. Would you deny your tyke the educational advantages of a home encyclopedia? It could, one day, mean the difference between a career scraping plates at Mamma Leone's and a successful group practice in obstetrics. Silly as this sounds, it seems to work like a charm. A few truly unlucky souls get clobbered twice: most publishers of adult encyclopedias will happily try to sell their customers a separate kiddies' edition.

If you're keen to provide a convenient source for the kids to plagiarize their homework assignments from, there's quite a choice of specially designed reference sets. Encyclopedias for children under eight resemble encyclopedias only in size and price. Better to buy individual books on topics that interest them (and you). The simplest real encyclopedias—Britannica Junior and the New Book of Knowledge—are meant for bright ten-year-olds. Both have flashy graphics and are exceedingly readable; both are edited to avoid the faintest hint of controversy about topics like sex, politics, and drugs. Since Britannica Junior sells for half as much as the $280 Book of Knowledge, it ranks as the lesser evil.

The heart of the children's encyclopedia market is in the next category up: sets meant to reach aggressive grade-schoolers and lazy high-school students. The Big Four—World Book (Marshall Field), Compton's (Britannica), Merit Students (Macmillan), and Encyclopedia International (Grolier)—are remarkably similar. World Book has a slight edge on quality of prose and content, Merit Students is prettiest. But Compton's is undoubtedly the best buy, costing $75 to $150 less than the competition.

Remember that none of these sets will satisfy the curiosity of adults who want to know more than the bare facts. Probably the most sensible strategy for pleasing everybody is to move up to the most streamlined of the adult encyclopedias, Collier's, move down to the Funk and Wagnalls supermarket special, or accept the limitations of the Columbia Encyclopedia.

• THE BEST EVIDENCE FOR THE EXISTENCE OF *ESP*

Extrasensory Perception has turned respectable. Consigned to the shadows for decades, believers in ESP—telepathy, clairvoyance, precognition—are now coming out of the closet. A 1973 survey by *New Scientist* magazine revealed that two thirds of the science professionals questioned either were certain ESP existed or thought it very likely. Even the American Association for the Advancement of Science, the scientific Establishment, has seen fit officially to recognize the value of research in parapsychology.

Whence this rapprochement with traditional science? Actually solid citizens have been flirting with ESP since the late nineteenth century: William James was president of the Parapsychological Association. There was nothing very scientific about the early parapsychologists, though. They spent most of their time sifting through tales of mediums and speculating about the message—all very fashionable, particularly in Victorian England. Entertainment/self-improvement for the middle classes.

Only in the 1930's, when academic psychologists attempted to expel the unworthy from the temple, did anyone test ESP in a serious fashion. William McDougall and Joseph Rhine started a parapsychology lab at Duke University, claiming early on that some experimental subjects could transmit and receive simple images from cards with a success rate that could not be explained by chance. Unfortunately, some of these famous experiments were compromised by sloppy controls and the lingering suspicion that the Duke fanatics cared too much about the outcome, that somehow they'd fudged it all.

Lots of experiments are conducted sloppily, of course; scientists prefer success to failure like the rest of us. But, whether or not the original Rhine results stand up, similar figure-identification telepathy experiments, completed in the 1950's by S. G. Soal at London University and others, have made the hard-line, it's-all-humbug view untenable. To deny their results is the equivalent of labeling dozens of otherwise respectable scientists as liars. There is little doubt that some people can transfer mental images to others miles away. No one has ever found a subject capable of receiving complex messages with consistent accuracy, though. The Amazing Karnak, alas, is a fraud.

Evidence for the existence of clairvoyance—receiving messages from inanimate objects without benefit of a transmitter—is almost as strong. Some subjects can guess the figure on the underside of a card with statistically impressive accuracy. In one convincing 1934 test, a graduate student at Duke, Hubert Pearce, was able to guess the figures on cards laid out, one by one, face down, in another campus building. Pearce was correct 288 out of 1,075 tries, when chance would have predicted just 215 (20 percent) right answers. Beating the odds by this margin may not seem like much, but the probability of doing that well on luck alone is about 1 in 25 million. Subsequent experiments at the University of Colorado in the late 1930's were equally impressive.

Yet more disturbing than the evidence for clairvoyance and telepathy are documented incidents of precognition, the anticipation of events that will take place in the future. After all, telepathy and clairvoyance don't really take all that much adjustment to accept: no one knows how they work, but the existence of senses little used (and of little use) shouldn't turn the universe upside down. The notion of predicting a future event, however, boggles the mind.

Two kinds of evidence for precognition have been offered. The first, soothsaying Jeanne Dixon style, or dreaming about the imminent death of a relative, for instance, doesn't have much punch, since there is no way to separate lucky guesses from the real thing. But the second type is more difficult to dismiss. In the 1930's Rhine and Soal, researching independently, found that some subjects were failing to guess card images in clairvoyance tests but were inadvertently predicting which cards would be chosen on the next random draw from the deck. Neither Rhine nor Soal was interested in publicizing this result, since it would have cast doubt on results less difficult to accept. Since the thirties, however, simple precognition experiments using virtually foolproof electronic random-event generators have produced evidence about equal in quality to telepathy and clairvoyance tests. The research appears free of logical errors; either precognition exists or the experimenters have been cheating.

If we suspend disbelief that some people can predict an event before it is actually caused, are we tossing away our sanity? Physicists aren't convinced, one way or the other, that precognition can be squeezed into their current views of the universe; it may be possible, at least in theory, to know about the future before it happens. Another solution to the puzzle is simpler. Perhaps precognition is mistaken for psychokinesis (PK), the ability to influence physical objects by thought alone. Guessing which card will be on top of the next shuffle may influence the shuffle. How PK might actually work is anybody's guess.

Should you wish to test your own capacity for precognition (and don't care to risk your days at the racetrack) a random-event generating machine is commercially available from Aquarius Electronics, P.O. Box 627, Mendocino, California 95460. The inventor, Russell Targ, calls it an ESP Teaching Machine, claiming the more you try, the better you get.

Who knows, maybe Karnak isn't a fraud.

• THE BEST EXERCISE

We don't mean the most fashionable exercise, though that's a natural misunderstanding these days. Sample dinner-party chatter among the Campari and soda crowd, and you'll hear more about the relative merits of Adidas and Converse than about Joseph Heller's angst or tax shelters in real estate. (For the record, squash is in; paddle tennis is very in. Tennis, cross-country skiing, and jogging still rate, but are slipping. Touch football? You must be kidding.)

Nor do we mean the exercise best designed to ward off sniggers around the pool. Exercise has less effect on shape than calories and heredity.

The main purpose of exercise is staying alive and remaining fit enough to enjoy it. Oddly enough, exercise for survival is the last thing on the minds of most physicians. Your average Grosse Pointe internist is happy to recommend polyunsaturated fats and high-fiber vegetables but doesn't have the foggiest idea about what exercise works or how

much is needed ("Try to get down to the club more often, but don't overdo it").

Herewith the gospel according to physiologists. Exercise keeps you alive by increasing the body's capacity to withstand occasional stress peaks and by decreasing the day-to-day load on circulation and respiration. Bulging muscles and flat bellies achieved through weight lifting, isometrics, or calisthenics look good but are no particular benefit to the heart, arteries, or lungs. The most painful exercise—sprints, intense tennis rallies, slalom skiing—puts tremendous stress on critical systems but has minimal conditioning effect because it lasts too short a time. Not to mention the fact that, if you are out of shape, that kind of exercise is plain dangerous. What works best are exercises that require real effort, yet are easy enough to keep doing for fifteen to thirty minutes at a crack. More precisely, the best exercise is one that gets your heart rate up to about 150 beats a minute and keeps it there for five to forty-five minutes (the longer the better). Such sustained stress increases lung efficiency, expands the network of arteries, and raises the red-cell count in your blood. It also lowers blood pressure and slows the heartbeat at rest.

By this test, cycling, jogging, and swimming all come off well, provided you are willing to work at them. How much work depends upon where you start. If your normal quota of exercise is opening the car door and punching the elevator "up" button, a shuffling twelve-minute mile is about par. College jocks can manage a mile in six or seven minutes, with effort but without pain. Given a little patience (about three months' worth) most anyone under sixty in reasonable health can trot the distance in eight minutes, or perform equivalent feats on wheels or water.

Remarkably few of us have the patience, of course.

Which leaves two options: fun-type weekend sports, and walking. Social exercises like handball, squash, tennis, skating, and skiing have some value if you do them long enough. A vigorous hour of tennis four days a week is better than doing nothing; once a week is as bad as nothing. The trick here is to count only the time on the job: mopping your brow between serves or admiring the view from the gondola lift isn't part of the hour. Walking briskly (over three miles an hour) strengthens the circulatory system, again provided you go far and frequently. A daily four miles, taken without stops, should keep the ambulance from the door.

• THE BEST EXPLANATION FOR THE STATE OF THE AMERICAN ECONOMY (CONTINUED)

Apparently frustrated by the anonymity of some of its most illustrious clients—William Miller, Mel Blanc, Frank Slayton, Carlton Fisk, George Gallup—American Express may be planning a new corporate strategy. California prison authorities report that Patty Hearst received a credit-card application in the mail just a few days after her arrest.

F THE BEST FAT FARM

What do Maurice Stans, Ava Gardner, O. J. Simpson, Jean Nidetch, and Mamie Eisenhower have in common? No, not the same hairdresser. They've all done stretches at one of the new health spas, otherwise known as fat farms. For reasons that escape us, times have never been better in calorieland. Whereas twenty years ago bulging matrons lacking will power had to beg for admittance to Maine Chance, the overweight affluent now have a choice of a dozen.

Fat farms come in all styles and shapes from Gracious Old South (the Greenhouse) to up-from-Seventh-Avenue (Harbor Island). No longer need petitioners cross the des-

ert to Phoenix if Honolulu (the Royal Door) or Palm Beach (the Palm Beach Spa) is more convenient. The only common denominator is money and, in one case (the Bermuda Inn), even the tab is no barrier.

In case you have something special in mind, we offer alternatives:

The Most Fashionable. Maine Chance, Elizabeth Arden's original, is the bastion of old Wasp money, just as it's been since 1934. For about $1,000 the wives, widows, and daughters of bloodless wealth can spend a restful week eating peapods off Wedgwood china and submitting to hot-wax treatments in the shadow of Camelback Mountain. For all its exclusivity, however, Maine Chance's deservedly dowdy image has turned off the under-sixty crowd. Your ambulatory rich and powerful now congregate at the Greenhouse (near Dallas) and the Golden Door (north of San Diego). The former, a subsidiary of Nieman-Marcus, specializes in Sun-Belt royalty plus regulars running from Annenberg to Windsor (Duchess of). Perhaps the most famous Greenhouse fraus are Lady Bird, Lynda, and Luci—all spend a minimum of a week here each year exercising ("Swing and Sway the Greenhouse Way"), dieting (800 to 1,000 calories), and developing makeup strategies with an expert from Charles of the Ritz. The highlight of the seven-day program is a shopping spree at Nieman-Marcus; charge cards are automatically provided for neophytes.

For hard-core chic, however, no spa can compete with the Golden Door. Besides being the most expensive—figure $1,400 plus change a week—the Golden Door attracts an eclectic clientele: Captains of Industry, Movie People, Politicians, and a trickle of Old Money. Eight weeks each year are reserved for men; another three are coed. While Maine

Chance and the Greenhouse made their reputations coddling the families of presidents, the Golden Door means business. Two hundred dollars a day buy more than just a lock on the refrigerator; a fixed regime of jogging, calisthenics, yoga, and water volleyball awaits the elite. Compensations include excellent food (all 900 calories of it), pink sweatsuits, and total privacy.

The Most Fun. The basic appeal of the classic fat farm is not weight loss but narcissistic regression. Elizabeth Arden perfected the formula, a combination of abstention, luxe, rigid scheduling, personal attention, and isolation. Most people love it, once they understand that all the privation is *for their own good.* Maine Chance still makes fewer concessions to the maturity of its clientele ("lights out at ten") than any other fat farm, but the Greenhouse isn't far behind.

By contrast, many new spas are just resort hotels with a health club and special diet menu. Here the subliminal pitch is to people who want to indulge without feeling guilty. Harbor Island Spa in Miami offers the standard fat-farm amenities—gym, massage, special diet foods, house sawbones—but doesn't insist anyone do anything disagreeable, such as exercise or diet.

La Costa, our favorite, is subtler. The beautifully equipped spa is a minor part of an enormous southern California resort/condominium complex. It's possible to lose weight and inches at La Costa, though not likely unless willpower is your forte. After a day in class ("Costa Curves, Costa Capers, Self-defense, Happy Feet, Guided Beachcombing"), spa inmates mingle with high-living vacationers, even eating in the same dining room. Nothing prevents the weak from recovering from Costa Capers or Happy Feet with a quick double Chivas at the bar. For that matter, no one will be the wiser if you skip the diet altogether and play tennis instead of Costa Curves.

The Most Effective. Suppose you really want to lose weight or break the three-vodka-martinis-with-lunch habit. Your surest bet is a wall-to-wall carpeted prison like the Golden Door, Greenhouse, or Maine Chance. Spas that treat you like an adult—the Royal Door, Palm-Aire (Pompano Beach, Florida), the Palm Beach—provide too many temptations. At any of the first three, you can reasonably expect to drop five pounds in a week; the Golden Door's exercise program is so rugged that you'll also trade in a few pounds of flab for muscle. How successfully you lay off the bottle depends on how determined you are to beat the system. All spas stop short of searching your luggage, or at least won't admit to it.

For dieters with more ambitious goals, there is the Bermuda Inn in southern California, right in the middle of the desert. The Bermuda Inn comes closer to a clinic than a spa, close enough to make you eligible for a tax deduction, provided you bring a note from your doctor. Guests are cajoled into eating as little as possible, always less than 400 calories per day; a physician prescribes vitamins and keeps track of your vital signs. Beyond that, you are free to do anything but swallow. This translates as swim, jog, watch television, play cards, and count prairie dogs. If you stick it out, the results can be phenomenal: up to ten pounds the first week, five each week thereafter. Cheaper than fasting in a hospital and safer than starving on your own.

• **THE BEST FRISBEE**

Not all frisbees are equal. For that matter, not all frisbees are Frisbees. The name is a trademark owned by the Wham-

O Company of San Gabriel, California. Your modern frisbee is a work of science and art, far from its humble origins before World War II as the container for Mr. Joseph P. Frisbie's commercial pies. Yalies, with nothing better to do, discovered that the inedible portion of Mr. Frisbie's creations had satisfactory aerodynamic qualities. Unlike the crude paint-can lid, a Frisbie tin hovered at slow speeds.

But enough history. Whatever their source, good frisbees are made of polyethylene and have a curved flight plate and tucked-in lip. All serious designs are based on the original Wham-O Pluto Platter, first produced in the mid-1950's. Attempts at non-cosmetic improvement include changing the scale, redistributing mass, and modifying the curve of the flight plate. Two decades of ad hoc experimentation (there are at least fifty models on sale in the United States) have proved that the original effort rates at least a B+.

Heavy frisbees (150 grams or more) work well in gusty winds but are a bear to catch. Large platters appear to have superior stability, but this is because they have proportionately more weight in the rim; the key is angular momentum. Variables determining velocity and maximum throwing distance are complex—the aerodynamic drag problem alone resists easy solution. With few exceptions, however, light-to-medium-weight frisbees have an edge in distance contests.

Hence the best frisbee depends upon priorities. For all-around play, where distance, catchability, hover, stability, and accuracy count, we go with the Pro. Wham-O's Professional Sport model checks in at 108 grams and 22.5 centimeters across. People with big hands generally prefer the Super Pro, with its extra weight and extra 5 centimeters in circumference.

For stability in wind, Wham-O's oversize, overweight disks, the Tournament and Master models, dominate. Given a choice, pick the 175-gram Tournament. For sheer distance, a strong player should opt for Concept Products All Star model. The All Star has an awkward profile, which goes to show that flight dynamics and intuition have little in common. Concept Products, incidentally, is the only manufacturer to compete seriously with Wham-O for the dollar (more often $2.25) of frisbee devotees. The fastest frisbee of them all is Wham-O's lithe Fastback; unfortunately the Fastback's profile renders it hopelessly unstable.

So much for serious frisbees. If your moral fiber has been so weakened that you no longer care how far or fast your frisbee travels, perhaps you are ready for the Explorer II from the L. M. Cox Company. Now, we have never seen one of these rare Cox beauties. However, a few words in this case are worth a thousand pictures. An ordinary frisbee does nothing but hover. Spin the Explorer II and centrifugal force automatically lights two tiny bulbs. Best for night play or during an eclipse of the sun.

• **THE BEST FUR**

If you take the word of Seventh Avenue, the recession's really over. Plain Republican cloth coats have retreated to Des Moines, routed by an army of fur, the more expensive the better. The big guns of haute couture—Calvin Klein, Bill Blass, Christian Dior—have turned their attention to mink pant suits and lynx ponchos. Even Halston has abandoned sensible Ultrasuede in favor of gray fox, fisher, and mole. What does all this mean for us peasants? Higher prices, almost certainly, but, on the bright side, sleek styles and plenty of variety.

Surely the most wonderful fur, now and forever, is sable. Sables, of a sort, are bred in Canada, but real sable is

Russian, exquisitely light and silky to the touch. The Soviets maintain a monopoly by refusing to export breeding stock; like good capitalists everywhere, they keep the price high by keeping production low. A full-length sable may require eighty to one hundred skins, at $100 to $400 per. It's no wonder that a dark-hue coat from the Tiffany of furriers, Ben Kahn, will set you back $30,000 to $50,000. In lighter shades—brown to amber—the price tag should be a gentler $10,000 to $20,000.

If you can't see your way clear to sell your soul for sable, perhaps you might consider a few eons in purgatory in exchange for a fisher. This lesser-known Canadian beast looks and feels like sable (well, almost) and retails for about half as much.

Back in the real world, the luxury fur preferred by a large majority is still mink, and for good reason. Russian broadtail lamb costs more, wears badly, and offers little protection from the cold. Chinchilla, which once rivaled sable in snob appeal, is out of fashion. Silver fox and Canadian lynx are beautiful furs, but their bulk usually makes them unflattering to the overfed.

Full-length, fully let out mink coats run from $2,000 to $12,000, depending on color, workpersonship, designer, and label. Dark natural shades (brownish-black is darkest) fetch a premium, but the cost difference is based only on scarcity, not durability or warmth. Like most furs, mink can be dyed either to imitate expensive natural colors or simply to achieve some designer's vision. There's nothing really wrong with dyed mink; some experts do claim, however, that dying reduces the life of the coat. Just make certain you aren't paying natural-color prices for imitation.

Mink from a famous house—Christie Brothers, Alixandre, Revillon, Ben Kahn—naturally costs more. We say

naturally because these are houses whose customers would be unhappy paying less. They're more likely to stock unusual colors and designs, the better to show the world you don't shop at Macy's. Workpersonship is also first rate. Chic adds about $2,000 to a standard $5,000 department-store mink, so ponder before you plunge.

Bargains in furs come in two forms. If status and style aren't your first priority, consider cheaper furs like raccoon and muskrat. No fur wears better or keeps you warmer than raccoon; choose among coats in natural brown or any of a half dozen dyed colors for $1,500 to $2,500. For even less ($1,200 to $2,000), there's the practical muskrat. It comes sheared and dyed, since *au naturel* muskrat looks too much like scruffy mink.

The alternative to a cheap common fur is a used snob fur from a resale shop. Secondhand mink, sable, chinchilla, lynx, and fox in excellent condition fetch only 30 to 50 percent of the new-coat price. This includes furs just a year or two old without the slightest sign of wear, last season's toys of the very rich, unappreciated gifts, and so on. Finding good value in used furs may be a shade harder, since it's difficult to comparison-shop, but in other respects there are no special secrets. A secondhand coat should be free of any visible damage to the pelt, any botched repairs, any clear sign of wear. Furs aren't like complex machinery—what you see is what you get.

THE BEST GERMAN RESTAURANT IN MILWAUKEE

Visiting firepersons are always trundled off to Mader's for the *Dunkelbier* and oompapa band. Some partisans make a fuss about the German pancake at Pandl's in suburban Whitefish Bay. But locals who know the difference between *Kasseler Rippchen* and *Königsberger Klops* prefer to stuff at Karl Ratzsch's.

Judging from the crowds that cram its huge, wood-paneled rooms seven nights a week, the quality of Ratzsch's cooking is the worst-kept secret in Milwaukee. Here you'll find the standard roast goose shanks, *Schnitzel à la Holstein,* beef *Rouladen,* and a sauerbraten many would kill for. Not to mention the house specialties: *Schnitzel à la Ratzsch* (with asparagus and crab legs), pork tenderloin cordon bleu, filet mignon with chicken livers and mushrooms. No human has ever finished a combination *Schlacht Platte* (bratwurst, smoked pork chops, potato dumpling, pork shank, pea purée, sauerkraut), but not for want of trying. Novices are often tempted by the liver dumpling soup (B−) or the lentil soup (A+) to start, though they soon learn they must pace themselves to save space for the cherry strudel with whipped cream.

The traditional accompaniment to one of these mittel European feasts is beer (and, later on, Maalox). But don't pass up the chance to order from one of the most extensive and reasonably priced wine lists in the world. Ratzsch's collection of German wines—about 130 estate labels, many in half bottles—represents every region and style. Just try finding a 1967 Marcobrunner Auslese or a 1953 Deidesheimer Trockenbeerenauslese in any other restaurant, or, for that matter, in any private cellar this side of the Rhine.

The real shock is the awesome variety of French and American wines, many at below wine store prices. Hundreds of classified-growth Bordeaux and *Grand Cru* Burgundies, rare Cabernet Sauvignons from Inglenook, Freemark Abbey, Robert Mondavi, and Beaulieu Vineyard, four California champagnes.

Drink a B. V. Cabernet Sauvignon Special Reserve 1968 or a Château Ducru-Beaucaillou 1961 before they are gone. But don't worry about finishing the beef *Rouladen* or potato dumpling—they'll be around forever.

• THE BEST GUIDE TO FRENCH RESTAURANTS

In 1966 Alan Zick, the chef of the Relais de Pourquerolles, committed suicide upon learning that his restaurant had been dropped by the Guide Michelin. Not everyone takes the famous red guide to French food this seriously, but the blessing of the Michelin inspectors can turn an obscure bistro into a gastronomic temple (and back again) faster than you can say *"Feuilleté de ris de veau."*

Each spring, amateur and professional eaters around the world await the new edition for word of their favorites. The 1976 guide awarded just seventeen restaurants the coveted three stars, neither promoting nor demoting a single establishment in the class. Michelin never justifies ratings and entertains no appeals. Yet the red book's conservatism, honesty, and general reliability rendered it untouchable for years, the first and last word on the subject.

No more. Critics claim the guide maintains its own enemies list, ignoring worthy restaurants out of spite or caprice. One such, Jacques Manière's Le Pactole in Paris, is viewed by many as one of the ten or fifteen best restaurants in France, yet it does not exist for Michelin. The same critics damn the Michelin for blocking the ascension of a new generation of chefs unwilling to pay obeisance at the shrine of Auguste Escoffier and Fernand Point. Specifically, the Michelin is skeptical of the rage for simplicity ("catch fish, slice fish, eat fish") and positively hostile to diet gastronomy.

If you've had enough of Michelin's bolts from Olympus or are simply curious about the competition, herewith a guide to the other guides.

**Guide Kléber*. The Avis of restaurant guides. Started in 1952 by the Kléber-Colombes company to offset rival Michelin's advantage in marketing tires, the Guide Kléber has never attempted to rate every single restaurant (or hotel) in France. It does not command a battalion of inspectors, relying instead on readers' reports and a network of informal contacts. Yet the editor, Jean Didier, has managed to scoop the Michelin on a dozen occasions. Didier champions no particular cause: the Kléber gives its highest rating to the most avant-garde of restaurateurs, Michel Guérard (Eugénie-les-Bains), and the most traditional, Lucas-Carton (Paris).

Limited coverage makes Kléber an inadequate substitute for Michelin if you find yourself in some isolated provincial town and must choose among available restaurants. Nor is Kléber as consistent as Michelin; among the clever discoveries each year are some that, on reflection, deserved their obscurity. Still, it's convenient to use—towns are grouped by region, and restaurants are displayed on accompanying regional maps—and fun to experiment with. Guidebook symbols are keyed in English, but Didier's occasional one-line comments are not translated.

Available in some U.S. big-city bookstores, newsstands

in France, or direct from the publisher, Guide Kléber, 6 villa Émile-Bergerat, 92200 Neuilly-sur-Seine.

Gault-Millau Guide. Henri Gault and Christian Millau like to shake things up. These two journalist/restaurant critics edit a chatty, catty, annual guide, as well as a monthly travel magazine for people who want to dine off the beaten *rue.* Well, that's the idea, anyway. But the guide has so much good gossip, and the pair are such publicity hounds, that a "discovery" in Paris is apt to be mobbed for months. Gault-Millau have a claim on the *nouvelle cuisine française,* that not very definable combination of simplicity and chic. They practically invented the Frères Troisgros (Roanne), and beat the bushes day and night for new culture heroes. Their latest: Freddy Girardet, chef/proprietor of the city hall restaurant in the Swiss village of Crissier, near Lausanne, which they rank as one of the seven best restaurants in the civilized (French-speaking) world.

Unfortunately, the Gault-Millau is as untrustworthy as it is interesting. These are the kind of Frenchman who will someday discover Nathan's Famous hot dog and solemnly declare it the eighth wonder of the universe. Another drawback: the reviews are in an idiomatic French that can't be translated with a pocket dictionary.

Available at newsstands in France or, if you must, try writing the gang at 210 rue du Faubourg St. Antoine, 75012 Paris.

***Guide Auto Journal.** No one ever seems to mention this nineteen-year-old guidebook, but in our experience it's the best. The Guide Auto Journal, sponsored by Uniroyal, reviews about 1,900 restaurants; 1,500 are included for their modest prices (this year the cut-off was five dollars per person), while the rest represent the editors' choice of the 400 best restaurants in France, regardless of cost. Each capsule review includes recommended dishes, wine and cheese specialties, comments on service and atmosphere. The French is elementary, but even if you can't read the text, the accompanying symbols are easy to figure out.

What is really special about the Guide Auto Journal is the critical judgment of the editors. Restaurants are rated on their merits, not to prove a point, reward friends, punish enemies, or shock readers. The editors understand that la Pyramide (Vienne) is the best restaurant in France even though it has become unfashionable; they also understand that Paul Bocuse (Lyons) is not far behind, in spite of the fact that it has become fashionable. Fine but flawed Parisian restaurants like Vivarois, Lucas-Carton, and Maxim's receive their just due.

Available at newsstands in France or by mail: 43 boulevard Barbès, 75880 Paris.

 THE BEST HOTEL

You might think that grand hotels have had their day, that inheritance taxes and college tuition have polished off the leisure class, leaving no one to foot the bill for linen bedsheets and wall-to-wall service. Such thoughts usually surface during the midnight search for the ice machine in some desolate airport Hilton Inn, or while cursing the busted cable TV in your regulation cracker-box HoJo.

Actually, nothing could be further from the truth. Their names and faces may change, but we will have the rich always with us. More important, the world is full of expense-account travelers who act like rich people whenever they can get away with it. From Beverly Hills to Quito to Nairobi to Hong Kong, luxe is available for the paying. Even in places where the water is poisonous, the air force is Russian-trained, and the natives eat manioc root for breakfast, chances are the local Intercontinental has thermostatically controlled air conditioning and a French chef in the kitchen.

Styles move with the times, of course. The new hotels are larger and more impersonal, the rooms may all look the same, and the bills may be printed by computer—which may not be all bad, since it's hard to sleep in more than one room at a time anyway, and computers are generally more accurate than clerks. But for those who object to progress, per se, we've divided the categories:

Grand Tradition. These are the places where the doormen dress up like Guatemalan generals, special rooms are set aside for personal maids, and the cashier's window is all but invisible. Such hotels don't exist in democratic America, except in modified versions. Give honorable mention to the Ritz-Carltons in Montreal and Boston, the Carlyle and Pierre in New York, the Westgate in San Diego, the Madison in Washington, the Whitehall in Chicago. Here you can expect good taste, good service, and the blessed absence of conventions.

Only in Europe, however, is it possible to find elegant hotels where time stopped in 1910. Switzerland has the Richemond in Geneva and the Dolder Grand in Zurich. The latter crowns a hillside above the city as if on perpetual guard duty for the anonymous billions stashed below. A Gobelin hangs in the main salon; the chef smokes his own salmon. Vienna has one hotel, the Imperial, that exudes the same dignified presence without similar benefit of topography. The secret is nineteenth-century opulence artfully masking twentieth-century Teutonic efficiency.

In London, there's Claridge's, with instantaneous room service around the clock and suites containing $50,000 worth of antiques; the Dorchester, catering to wealthy travelers who like their luxury up front; the tiny Connaught, all mahogany and tradition. IRA bombers and militant unions haven't made a dent in their façades.

In Rome, the choice is either the Hassler or the Grand. The Grand has been damaged less by chain ownership than by its popularity with the Beautiful People; still, it's just fine, unless you object to rococo overkill. Diffident types prefer the smaller (hundred-room) Hassler, with its Louis Quinze furniture and view from the Spanish Steps. Neither should be compared to Venice's Gritti Palace, though, the hotel with the most beautiful interiors on the continent. The Ritz in Madrid comes a close second.

We have, of course, saved the best for last. Paris has more grand hotels than any other city, and the grandest among these is—need one state the obvious?—the Ritz. The Crillon, Plaza-Athénée, and Meurice are not hardship posts. But the Ritz is special. Created in 1898 by César Ritz, it has defined luxury ever since. The hotel entrance is hidden along the stone façade of the traffic-choked Place Vendôme, though most of the 160 rooms face landscaped interior courtyards; before M. Ritz purchased the building, it had been the townhouse of the Duc de Lauzun. Auguste Escoffier transformed *haute cuisine* in the kitchens of the Ritz, which still maintains one Michelin star. During the summer, guests may dine in the formal Louis XV room, in the bourgeois Espadon, or outside in the gardens. If the price of a room ($80 and up), or a meal (about $40 per person), is out of range, try the Ritz bar. Fifty years post-Hemingway, it's still the place in Paris to see assorted literary types, bored billionaires, and hangers-on.

Chrome and Glass. Hotels don't have to be Edwardian palaces to be good. Personally, we are suckers for the indoor pool at the Paris Sofitel, with its poolside vistas of the city, or the great interior courtyards of the Atlanta Hyatt Regency and the other Portman extravaganzas in San Francisco and Houston. Los Angeles has the charming excess of the Beverly Wilshire (Jacuzzis in the bathrooms, leather wallpaper in the bar) and the *2001* efficiency of the Century Plaza. For sheer glitter there's the Othon Palace in Rio, La Bonaventure in Montreal, the Okura in Tokyo, the El Presidente in Mexico City, or the Mandarin overlooking Hong Kong harbor.

Yet none is quite in the class of the new Berkeley in London, the only aggressively modern hotel that maintains nineteenth-century service standards. Opened a few years ago, the Berkeley possesses a penthouse swimming pool with retractable roof, a roman bath and sauna, a tiny movie theater, a restaurant/discothèque complete with waterfall. Somehow this is all pulled off with good taste, the flash coexisting peacefully with an otherwise understatedly elegant small hotel.

Good taste does have a way of lightening the wallet, and it's no surprise that the Berkeley is one of the most expensive places in the world to spend a night. Assume $100 for a room, perhaps three times that for a suite.

• THE BEST HUBERT HUMPHREY LINE

In response to a wire-service request for comment on Sara Jane Moore's and Squeaky Fromme's near-misses: "There are too many guns in the hands of people who don't know how to use them."

J THE BEST JUG WINE

Not all changes are for the worse. A half-dozen years ago, importers were riding the crest of a snob-wine boom of unprecedented proportions. Great French growths, ounce for ounce, became more valuable than silver bullion, and all over the globe corporate speculators fought for the privilege of stocking up on leftover châteaux at $80 a case. Three enormous grape harvests, one nasty recession, and assorted bankruptcies later, snob wines are out and ex–wine snobs are busy extolling the virtues of the Gallo Brothers.

Happily there's no way multinational corporations or Japanese steel barons could run up the price of everyday drinking wines, even if they wished to. Garden-variety jug wines are made from high-yield, hot-weather grapes that can be grown practically anywhere the sun shines, from California to Algeria to Turkey. Whenever another 10,000 consumers make the switch from Dr. Pepper, the folks at Gallo plant a few hundred more acres or send out for a few hundred tons of fresh grape juice. The real trick is to find the jug that makes the switch worth while.

First things first. No wine under $4 a half gallon, no matter how beautiful the container or how slick the ads, is a match for quality California, French, German, Spanish, or Italian wine. Jug wine is never subtle—subtlety requires better grapes and more care than any producer can afford to invest. Jug wine never benefits from aging in the bottle. On the contrary, age is the enemy of inexpensive wines, red or white. A really first-rate jug resembles the wine served from kegs in country restaurants all over the world—light, tart, refreshing, low in alcohol.

Many brands fail the test on purpose. Primarily, this is a matter of economics. Good country wines can't sit around in a warehouse for two months or cross the Atlantic in a freighter hold at 110 degrees without risk of spoilage. But add enough chemical preservatives and sugar, or raise the alcohol level, and your average jug is content to collect dust on the shelf practically indefinitely. Besides, market researchers are convinced that you like your fermentables soft and sweet (the code word is *mellow*). As the theory goes, young moderns have been too corrupted by Ripple and Cherry Kijafa to like a wine that is dry or acidic.

If your palate has escaped destruction by the purveyors of pop wine, but you can't afford to sip the very best, a few strategic hints on jug selection:

—Avoid the super-cheapies, half gallons under $1.99. They aren't *all* terrible, just most of them.

—You probably assume jugs with varietal names (Zinfandel, Cabernet, Grenache) will be better than fake Burgundies or made-up names, but often as not you'd be wrong. California varietals in the jug price range average neither better nor worse than their imprecisely labeled cousins.

—Never buy a jug that you can't finish within a few

days; jug wines decline rapidly after exposure to air. Re-bottle leftovers in small screw-top soda bottles and refrigerate.

—Forget the rules about serving red wine at room tem-

perature. After a light chill, most inexpensive reds lose nothing but their sweetish beginning and raisin-like aftertaste.

—When you find the jug wine of your dreams, pray the producer doesn't alter the formula. Many brands change flavor every year or two, as the winery experiments with new techniques, finds a less expensive source of grapes, or aims to please a different segment of the market. The most famous casualty: Gallo Hearty Burgundy, which seems to get mellower every year.

—As mentioned before, place names like Burgundy don't mean much on California or Spanish jugs. Still, they give some hint of what the winery intended. "Claret" means dry red; "Burgundy" and "Chianti" are less dry and perhaps a touch fruity. Among whites, "Chablis" is dry, "Rhine" is sweet and low in acid, "Sauterne" is just plain sweet.

—While exceptions are numerous, California reds are better buys than European; Spanish, French, and Italian labels excel in white wines.

Our favorite jugs (this month, anyway) are Gallo Barbera (red), the Italian brand Marino Frascati (white), and Inglenook Navalle Rosé. The Inglenook rosé, incidentally, doesn't have much taste but is an eminently satisfactory thirst-quencher on a hot night.

THE BEST KITCHEN KNIFE

It should be easy to buy a good knife, but it isn't. We don't know why, but here's a theory. Most knives come as wedding presents, and everybody knows it's the thought that counts. The rest come from mail-order houses with the guarantee that they can be sharpened on the back of a plate. Would you sell a good knife to anybody dumb enough to believe that?

First, the basics. No single knife can do everything well. The compleat chef, or anyone else let loose in the kitchen, needs a minimum of three different kinds: a heavy chef's knife for chopping, a long thin slicing knife for cutting meat, and a three- to four-inch paring knife for peeling and dicing. Some sets include a long serrated knife necessary for slicing bread and/or a medium-length utility knife to help justify the price tag.

Brands vary greatly both in construction quality and design. Quality of construction is most obvious in the handle. Plastic handles wear better than wood but become slippery at the sight of raw meat. Better to opt for rosewood or non-slip-finish aluminum. The knife tang—the metal extension of the blade that binds blade to handle—should run the full length of the handle. This improves balance and decreases the probability that the handle will shatter the first time it receives a workout. On all good knives the tang is attached with rivets rather than glue.

Solingen, Sheffield, and Sabatier mean less than you think. The first two are merely the names of medieval European metal-working centers. Would you read a book because it was printed by Gutenberg? Sabatier is a French trademark; however, it is licensed to dozens of manufacturers producing good, bad, and indifferent cutlery.

The hardest part of picking a knife is picking the blade type. Stainless steel containing chromium stays pretty and stays sharp for weeks. Once the edge goes, though, it's probably gone forever. Good stainless is extremely hard to resharpen, requiring more patience than you are likely to have. High-carbon steel, on the other hand, turns grungy black, rusts at the mere mention of water, and loses its edge in short order. Professionals, however, use it almost exclusively because carbon blades sharpen easily and well.

We recommend a better mousetrap, the new "no-stain" high-carbon blade. This is exactly what it sounds like, stainless steel with a high carbon content, soft enough to sharpen quickly with a chrome-steel or ceramic tool, and capable of holding a good edge. The brand we've used is called Friodur, made by Henckel. It never gets quite as sharp as a fine-standard high-carbon blade (say, the Professional-brand Sabatier) but you'll probably never notice. The plastic-impregnated wood handle is supposed to be dishwasherproof. Pass by that provocation, though, if you can. Putting a good knife in a dishwasher is like taking a Norell to the laundromat.

- **THE BEST KITE**

If you think kites are made to get nine-year-olds out of the house on Saturday morning, consider yourself dated. Kiting is in, very in. Forty to fifty million kites are now sold each year, and a surprising percentage end up in the hands of people who used to spend their spare time polishing backhands or checking out the scene at Bloomingdale's.

Even *Town and Country,* that last refuge for Old Money, recently saw fit to sandwich a guide to kites between the Alfa Romeo and Halston ads. Fittingly, the article featured a hand-painted, six-foot beauty from Japan that retails for $500. But nice kites come as cheap as $3. Among the possibilities:

Ace. An ideal beginner's kite, and one of the best all-round, the Ace is typical of new delta-wing designs pioneered by Al and Betty Hartig in Nantucket. Modest size delta-wings in cotton cloth or plastic are cheap (the Ace is about $10), durable, and stable once aloft. But most of all they are easy to launch, requiring just a light breeze and a flick of the forearm. Compare the classic diamond-shaped paper kites of the fifties, the kind nobody's father could ever get off the ground. Flat, diamond shapes are still around, but are inferior in just about every way to modern designs.

Tetra. A commercial kit version of the advanced box kite invented by Alexander Graham Bell. Bell was interested in finding the most efficient rigid shape, the shape that would support the most weight per pound of kite. His four-sided tetrahedron was a big improvement over simple boxes, but requires enormous size to reach maximum efficiency. Bell once actually flew a 3,393-cell tetrahedral design, one of the largest kites ever built.

The simple Tetra ($7) is too small to fly in light winds, doing well only in medium breezes. SuperTetra ($20), four times as large, is still meant only for stronger winds. Their real virtue is aesthetic—never has a more beautiful shape flown.

Incidentally, big cellular kites once held all the records for lifting capacity and altitude. This fact was not lost on Orville and Wilbur Wright, who modeled their Kitty Hawk plane after box kites used by the weather bureau to carry instruments above the clouds. A train of nineteen cellular kites reached an altitude of 35,000 feet over Portage, Indiana, in 1969.

Fighters. Certain competitive types may wonder what to do after the kite goes up, once the risk of myocardial infarction at the launching has been eliminated. Setting endurance records isn't all that appealing—who has 168 hours to waste?—and staring at the clouds has its limits.

One answer is the fighter kite, an idea that's been kicking around Asia for ten centuries. Fighter kites are light and highly maneuverable; with practice, you can make them bank or dive with a light tug on the line. In Korea and

India, hobbyists do battle with their fighters, attempting to knock each other from the sky by crossing lines. In deference to high American kite prices, the contest has been modified: competitors use their kites to demolish helium target balloons dancing in the wind.

Indian fighters made of paper ($3 to $6) are more practical than the Korean variety, since they can do their tricks even in very light breezes. More durable, and almost as light as the Indian imports, are American imitations (around $8) made of a metallized plastic called Mylar. Mylar fighters aren't quite as maneuverable but can be flown in high winds that would tear apart the ordinary Indian paper fighter.

Exotic Shapes. Lifelike kites like the German-manufactured Eagle ($7) generate curiosity and aggression from local birds with a strong sense of territorial rights. Unlike the Eagle, however, unusual kites are generally difficult to launch and weak on maneuverability once they're up. The Japanese Centipede ($7), one of the nicest, consists of a dozen small paper disks connected by flexible bamboo sticks. If you are lucky enough to get the Centipede airborne, you'll see the eight-foot kite slink like a serpent. Another exotic shape, the Ghost Clipper ($20), looks very much like a Clipper Ship in full sail, if and when it leaves the earth.

The best kite, though, is more than just another pretty face. The revolutionary Para-Foil, invented by Dominia Jalbert, has no rigid frame. It holds its shape through air pressure alone, puffing out like a wind sock. What makes Para-Foil special, apart from durability and superb flying stability, is its mind-boggling weight-lifting capacity; a ten-pound Para-Foil can carry a 150-pound object in a stiff breeze.

Such extraordinary lift may make it possible to use giant Para-Foils as emergency rescue gliders for airplanes or as cheap vehicles for returning astronauts. Small versions in plastic (good for nothing in particular except kiting) can be purchased for $25 to $250.

Para-Foils and all the other kites mentioned are available by mail from Go Fly a Kite Store, Inc., 1434 Third Avenue, New York, New York 10028.

 THE BEST MEDICAL SCHOOL

Ask an M.D. who cares about such things, and chances are you'll be told Harvard or Johns Hopkins. Graduates from these two schools have the inside track on the most prestigious internships, and many carry this slight edge through their careers. That might not seem like much of an answer, but it's hard to find a better test.

With Ph.D.'s in physics driving hacks these days, medical schools can choose among the pick of the undergraduate litter. As a result, at least twenty universities run med programs with higher standards than any school decades ago. Less well known medical schools, like Rochester and the University of Washington, have gotten better faster than the old elite (Harvard, Hopkins, Yale, Columbia, Cornell, Penn), so the gap between very good and very best has narrowed considerably. Objective criteria for sorting them out are elusive.

Two sociologists, Peter Blau and Rebecca Margulies, tried the simplest approach: surveying people who ought to know. They asked medical school deans for a list of the five best schools, then ranked ten by the percentage of times each school made the deans' list. There were no surprises at the top: Harvard won easily, with Hopkins a distant second. The big shocks came later. Duke ranked third, the University of California at San Francisco and the University of Washington tied for eighth. Mighty Columbia barely managed tenth place, while Penn, Michigan, Mount Sinai, Cornell, Albert Einstein, NYU, Northwestern, Minnesota, and Dartmouth placed out of the money.

Of course, if you don't like the score, you can always change the rules. Good schools must have good students. Right? Virtually all medical schools require applicants to take the standardized Medical College Admissions Test (MCAT), and many publish the average scores of the students they admit. Unfortunately, some schools put their best foot forward, revealing only test results for selected sections of the four-part test, while a few very good schools —Harvard, NYU, Penn, George Washington, Yale, Dartmouth—coyly guard their reputations by not publicizing any numbers at all. For what it's worth, though, the University of California at San Francisco had the highest overall mean score (645) published in 1975, with U.C. at San Diego (640), Chicago (635), and Vanderbilt (630) close behind.

We think two other statistical measures might be more revealing: the percentage of recent graduates (classes of 1960 through 1969) who have become board-certified specialists, and the percentage of alumni/ae who are members of medical school faculties.

93

% BOARD-CERTIFIED SPECIALISTS

	%
TUFTS	59.6
CORNELL	59.0
COLUMBIA	58.9
PENN	58.4
JOHNS HOPKINS	58.3
HARVARD	57.9
WASHINGTON, ST. LOUIS	57.7
VANDERBILT	56.0
EINSTEIN	54.6
NYU	54.1

% MEDICAL SCHOOL FACULTY

	%
CHICAGO	17.3
HARVARD	17.1
YALE	15.3
JOHNS HOPKINS	14.8
COLUMBIA	12.8
CORNELL	12.4
ROCHESTER	12.0
NYU	10.3
PENN	9.9
CASE WESTERN RESERVE	9.4

• THE BEST MINERAL WATER

Europeans drink mineral water because they think it has
curative powers somewhere between tetracycline and God.
French consumers lead the world, downing about thirty-five
quarts per liver each year, in the vain hope that Vichy,

Badoit, Evian, and so on, will neutralize the cumulative effects of alcohol and butterfat. Your Avenue Foch crowd swears by the slimming properties of Contrexéville, from the Vosges mountains. In deference to Food and Drug Administration rules, American water bottlers make no medicinal claims, but have still managed to triple sales since 1970. Perhaps it's the health scare that treated tap water contains traces of chemicals linked to cancer. Or maybe it's become chic to mix J & B with Perrier.

If you want to play the game, too, first you must learn the rules. *Artesian, mineral,* and *spring* water must be just what they say: H_2O plus assorted minerals added by nature. *Purified* on the label means the manufacturer has processed municipal tap water, usually removing chlorine and other impurities, possibly adding some trace minerals for that certain zing. *Distilled* water is nearly pure water; drink it if you wish, but chances are you'll find it very boring.

European mineral waters are all bottled at the source, while the native stuff is probably hauled to bottlers in tank cars to save transportation costs. Some bottled water is fizzy. If the label says *naturally carbonated,* the processer has gone to the trouble of collecting escaping gas from the spring and reinjecting it into the bottle. Otherwise, bubbly waters are manufactured with commercial carbon dioxide, like Dr. Pepper or Tab.

If you drink water to cure sinus headaches or tennis elbow, consult a local witch doctor or ouija board for the brand of choice (European health freaks seem to favor brands loaded with sulphur). If taste is your only motive for shelling out thirty-five cents to five dollars a gallon, ponder the ratings below. For comparison, we've thrown in Canada Dry Club Soda and New York City tap water (the nation's best).

RATING	BRAND	COMMENT

Carbonated

VG	Badoit Mineral Water	Faintly fizzy; subdued mineral taste with little aftertaste.
G	Perrier Mineral Water	Probably the most popular imported brand. Heavy natural carbonation. Can't be beat as a mixer.
F	Canada Dry Club Soda	Extremely small, long-lasting bubbles. The fizz dominates the flavor, which is probably just as well.
P	Mattoni Water	From the Kyselka Spring in Czechoslovakia. Lightly carbonated. Slight gagging quality. Maybe it's the Vanadium (0.0006 mg per liter) or the Hydroarsenate (0.074 mg per liter).
P	Saratoga Vichy Water	Medium carbonation, distinctly salty. For what it's worth, the only naturally carbonated American water.
P	Appollinaris Mineral Water	The most popular mineral brew in West Germany. Medium carbonation, distinctly metallic aftertaste.

RATING	BRAND	COMMENT
P	San Pellegrino Mineral Water	If you prefer your water to be Italian. Very lightly carbonated, faintly sulphury aftertaste.
VP	Vichy Célestins	A ringer for Alka-Seltzer Gold. Don't confuse it with Saratoga Vichy. Well, on second thought, who cares.

Non-Carbonated

RATING	BRAND	COMMENT
VG	Great Bear Spring Water	Available in the Northeast. The platonic spring water: no aftertaste, nice zing.
VG	Deep Rock Artesian Water	From an artesian well near Denver; sold in the West. Very similar to Great Bear.
G	New York City tap water	All are very slightly mineraly. And all are free of any foreign taste. If you can tell the difference blindfolded, you've got a mass spectrometer for a tongue. Buy by price alone.
G	Contrexéville Natural Mineral Water	
G	Evian Spring Water	
G	Mountain Valley Water	
G	Deer Park Spring Water	

• THE BEST MOSQUITO REPELLENT

Deerflies work on the slash-and-run principle: land, rip through the victim's skin, slurp up some blood, buzz off. By comparison, the gentle mosquito is nature's pickpocket, counting on surprise and deception rather than brute force and speed. First she (only females indulge) penetrates the skin with a hair-fine hollow needle, then she injects an enzyme solution to prevent blood clotting, drinks her fill, and tactfully withdraws. Save for a skin reaction to the anti-clotting enzyme, most people would never know they'd been visited.

Of course, it's the allergic skin reaction that makes the garden-variety North American mosquitoes such pests and supports a battalion of researchers looking for the perfect repellent. Until very recently, the search has been trial and error. Before World War II, the only compound known to ward off insects was citronellol, an oil extracted from tropical plants. Then danger from malaria-carrying mosquitoes during the war pushed the army into a massive testing program—25,000 chemicals were tried before a few effective non-toxic ones were found.

Scientists had always assumed that bugs were attracted or repelled by smell. Actually, nature is much fancier. Mosquitoes are interested in odor—they seem to like aftershave—but their guidance system works mainly through carbon dioxide, temperature, and humidity. They follow warm, wet, CO_2-laden air currents to the source: a breathing, warm-blooded animal, they hope. That's why a good sweat seems to attract every insect in town. Insect repellents don't really repel, they just jam the tiny sensors that pick up humidity. The mosquito heads for her target, sometimes even landing, but flies away from the tastiest meal because her wetness sensors have ceased to respond.

The standard jammer found in every commercial repellent is N,N Diethyl-meta-toluamide, or Deet for short. Deet fools mosquitoes in concentrations one thousandth as strong as citronellol and rarely irritates skin. Anti-bug sprays usually don't last as long as creams, foams, or liquids, possibly because they don't contain as much of the active ingredient. Read the labels: other things being equal, the percentage of Deet is a good indicator of how well the repellent will work. At least three brands, Cutter Insect Repellent, 6-12 Plus, and Deep Woods Off, have added a mess of new organic chemicals to increase the protection time from a single dose. Remember too that the effect of chemical repellents is extremely localized—any patch left uncoated is vulnerable.

O THE BEST ODDS ON THE NEXT NUCLEAR POWER

No doubt, since India blew a hole in the Rajasthan desert in 1974 with a fifteen-kiloton "nuclear device" you've been wondering who would be next to join the club. Herewith the morning line:

Pakistan (3–1). Pakistan may be short on know-how but it is long on motivation. India claims it dug that crater in the desert for peaceful purposes, but no one has yet found a peaceful purpose for nuclear explosives. The Pakistanis had the foresight not to sign the Nuclear Non-Proliferation Treaty in 1968, so a nuke of their own would violate no international agreement.

Just about anybody can build a crude bomb these days, given a sufficient amount of the right kind of uranium (U-235) or plutonium. The major powers, however, aren't about to offer preprocessed fixings to Pakistan, so they will have to do it the hard way. Uranium nuclear reactor fuel (which Pakistan does have, courtesy of Canada) yields small quantities of waste plutonium. Once the Pakistanis obtain the equipment to purify these plutonium wastes, they will be in business. Without foreign help, plutonium processing will take quite a while, but help could be secretly forthcoming from any of a half-dozen Western European countries.

Israel (5–1). Israel probably has a few plutonium bombs ready to go, constructed with reprocessed waste from its super-secret Dimona reactor. It doesn't admit having reprocessing capability, but doesn't deny it either. The indirect evidence is convincing, however: Israel has pressed the United States for Pershing missiles, capable of hitting targets deep into Egypt and Syria. Pershings are worthless for any purpose other than nuclear bomb delivery, since they could miss their targets by a quarter mile or more.

Whether Israel will be tempted to demonstrate one of its weapons in the next few years is unclear. A test bomb would make the United States very angry and put pressure on the Soviets to supply Syria with an equalizer. Still, Israeli hawks argue that a show of zeal now could make the United States worry less about pleasing the oil sheiks and more about how to handle their unpredictable ally.

Iran (10–1). At the moment the Shah is far behind in the nuclear sweepstakes, but determined to catch up. Iran is spending lavishly on nuclear power reactors (purchased in the United States), which will provide a satisfactory supply of plutonium waste within a decade. More important, the Iranians are making friends with the French and West Germans, trading crude oil for nuclear capability. The United States may be fussy about helping the Shah rule the world; France and Germany have no such scruples.

Argentina/Brazil (15–1). Some smart money is riding on Argentina to defy the odds and go nuclear next. It has everything it needs, including a plutonium processing plant and an ample supply of plutonium garbage from fission power plants. All Argentina really lacks is a reason to defy international public opinion.

Brazil could furnish the reason. While currently behind Argentina in nuclear capability, Brazil is itching to make it clear that it is a nation to be reckoned with. The bomb may eventually be more of a liability than an asset (military spending would drain resources away from the rapidly expanding economy), but don't count on rationality to carry the day. West Germany has agreed to supply additional reactors and a reprocessing plant.

Egypt (15–1). Unlike Israel, Egypt is far from possessing a nuclear weapon. The United States has promised to supply President Sadat with a big power reactor, an offer also made to the Israelis. Sympathizers claim that the agreement includes strict safeguards, but chances are still fair that the Egyptians will find a way to divert some plutonium for military use. With or without American help—the French are always willing to lend a hand—Egypt could probably manage a nuclear weapons program. If Israel officially unveils its bomb, change that "probably" to "certainly."

Taiwan (15–1). The Nationalist Chinese are quite far along in nuclear technology, possessing adequate plutonium generating capacity and even a working plutonium processing plant. Hence, in theory, nothing stands in their way. In practice, however, politics counts too. Taiwan ratified the Non-Proliferation Treaty long ago under U.S. pressure. If and when the United States and Japan abandon the Nationalists completely, they may feel the need for their own nuclear deterrent.

Sweden, Switzerland, Canada, West Germany, Italy, and Japan (100–1). All are perfectly capable of building a bomb within a year or two of the decision, but none is likely to make the first move.

South Korea, Indonesia, and Australia (200–1) would all have to break substantial technological barriers, but all have the minimum scientific capacity and would be able to purchase what they can't manufacture.

• **THE BEST ORCHID**

Plenty to choose from, since there are over 25,000 identified natural species and innumerable greenhouse hybrids. Of course, most orchids are just pretty, but a few have special talents:

—Some *Ophrys* varieties look remarkably like flies or bumblebees. This is no accident, since they also produce a scent that drives male flies and bumblebees mad with desire; the insects spread pollen while slaking their lust.

—Other species practice other deceptions in the same cause. The *Coryanthes* (bucket orchid) maintains a tiny pool of liquid in the base of its flower. Visiting insects slip on the lip of the pool, take a bath, and then inadvertently collect pollen on their wet bellies as they struggle out the back door. The *Catasetum* leave nothing to chance, spraying anything that brushes their antennae with a blast of pollen.

—The *Rhizanthella,* a pale pinkish-white orchid, distinguishes itself by existing entirely underground. All its nutrients are obtained from the soil, rendering it independent of sunlight.

—The *Vanilla* orchid—yep, you guessed it—manufactures vanilla flavoring. Actually, there are almost seventy species in the genus *Vanilla.* The seed pods of one particularly boring-looking species, *Vanilla planifolia,* are harvested and then fermented to obtain vanilla flavoring.

—*Grammatophyllum* have hefty appetites. Given enough time, they can grow to the size of trees, occasionally reaching twenty-five feet high. The flowers of these champion species, incidentally, are just four to six inches across.

Actually, there is much more to recommend orchids than such Disney World eccentricities and, contrary to myth, many varieties make excellent house plants. Nearly two hundred years ago, the first tropical orchids were imported by English aristocrats with time on their hands and money to burn. Orchids became a hobby for the upper classes, reaching an apogee of popularity during the late Victorian era; auction prices for rare species occasionally topped $5,000. Although some orchids are still very expensive and some are impossible to raise outside greenhouses, hundreds of beautiful varieties cost less than $25 delivered full-grown from a commercial nursery, and require about as much care as a philodendron from the A&P. Orchids grow wild all over the world, some individual species adapting to wide ranges of temperatures, humidity, and sunlight. Where nature hasn't cooperated, botanists have employed coercion, crossing species to obtain handsome flowers that can stand the rigors of living above the dishwasher.

Popular genera within reach of the brown thumb set

include *Cattleya, Paphiopedilum,* and *Phalaenopsis.* (*Cattleya* should ring a bell for lit. majors: in *Swann's Way,* Swann called making love "doing a cattleya," honoring the memory of the orchids Odette wore in her cleavage.) Al-

most all corsage orchids are *Cattleya* species, since they are flashy, sturdy, and easy to grow. They thrive without special pampering, given a reasonable amount of sun, minimal humidity and a 10-to-20-degree temperature drop at night.

Paphiopedilum, sometimes incorrectly called *Cypripeduim,* are distinguished by their waxy luminescent flowers with pouch-like appendages. Orchid collectors are big on "paphs" at the moment, rekindling an enthusiasm that was widespread in Europe until the 1930's. Most hybrid species tolerate low light levels well and aren't very fussy about temperature or humidity.

Phalaenopsis aren't as easy, but their simple flat-petaled flowers are so attractive that it is worth a try. They like a warm daytime temperature and a dip into the fifties at night, lots of humidity, little sun.

Our first choice, though, is none of these. The *Odontoglossum* has a well-earned reputation as a bitchy orchid genus, seemingly unable to adapt to less than perfect conditions. Dominant varieties from the Andes of Ecuador require moderation in all things—soft sunlight, daytime temperatures between 65 and 75 degrees, substantial humidity. Luckily, though, one group of *Odontoglossum,* tiger orchids from Central America, are much more adaptable. Gold and red and brown tigers usually settle for what you offer—a kitchen window or an outside garden in the Sun Belt.

Whatever you choose, start raising orchids with plants ready to yield flowers. Seedlings are less expensive but take several years to bloom (or may never bloom at all). Pros recommend shopping at a specialized orchid nursery; florists and local plant shops rarely know what they are selling or how to take care of it. With thousands of species and hybrids around, good advice is critical. Specialized mail-order orchid houses should serve almost as well as a local greenhouse. Reputable ones won't knowingly sell you plants you can't raise, or ship plants that can't take the trauma. Try writing the following for catalogues: Fred Stewart, Inc. (1212 East Las Tunas Drive, San Gabriel, California 91778), Orchids by Hauserman (P.O. Box 363, Elmhurst, Illinois 60126), Ilgenfritz Orchids (P.O. Box 1114, Monroe, Michigan 48161).

THE BEST-PAID ATHLETE

Professional athletes, at least the ones at the very top, have done nicely ever since the invention of network television. But only in the past few years could a twenty-game winner's right arm become more valuable than an acre of prime real estate on Fifth Avenue. With the help of the federal courts, star performers have been able to write salary contracts in the range of multinational corporation executives'. Any old NBA guard who can play defense pulls down a good six figures.

The very best paid athlete, of course, is not on salary. Muhammad Ali made $8,500,000 piecework, defending his title four times, in 1975. A good chunk of that went for expenses, but then Ali picked up a little extra doing television commercials. Among salaried jocks, Pelé, Pepsi Cola's contribution to the New York Cosmos, earns the most. The actual figure is in doubt, though it's probably somewhere between $780,000 and $1,566,000, depending upon which sports page you read. Contracts in these ranges are written with one eye on publicity and the other on the Internal Revenue Service; usually only the lawyers know for sure.

As a bonus, here are a few other pre-tax salaries for comparison: Julius Erving, $600,000; Kareem Abdul-Jabbar and George McGinnis, $500,000; Joe Namath, $450,000; Walt Frazier and Catfish Hunter, $400,000; Arthur Ashe and Angel Cordero, $300,000; Tom Seaver, a mere $225,000.

• THE BEST PIANO

Forget the image of Eastern European refugees in cheerful workshops lovingly snipping felt, tightening pegs, and matching veneers. Piano-making is big business, an assembly-line enterprise run by engineers, accountants, and systems analysts. Like Porsche or Pepperidge Farm, piano manufacturers thrive on the Santa's workshop illusion, but the bottom line is all Teflon, inventory control, and advertising penetration. Most first-rate piano manufacturers have been bought out by conglomerates or mass-market producers. CBS owns Steinway; Mason and Hamlin, Knabe, Chickering, Steck, and Weber were swallowed up by the Aeolian Corporation, which was in turn consumed by Winter and Company. Bösendorfer is a subsidiary of Kimball International, Inc., while Bechstein found a home in the Baldwin organization.

Nowhere is it written, of course, that fine pianos can't be made by candidates for the Fortune 500; Pepperidge Farm whole wheat tastes pretty good even if it isn't baked in New

England farmhouses. In fact, the fate of the great trademarks in the hands of the philistines has varied considerably. Aeolian/Winter preserved the façade of independence for its prestigious subsidiaries, but little else. Mason and Hamlin, known for durability and tone quality and once considered America's best piano, is now merely acceptable. Chickering and Knabe (Mason and Hamlin's former competitors) met a similar end; they are satisfactory, mass-

produced instruments with no special character.

The impact of CBS on Steinway is uncertain. Everyone agrees that the Steinway has fallen; just how far remains a matter of controversy. Owners complain about premature wear in Steinway's moving parts and the indifferent quality of its service network. Yet Steinways are still endorsed, without cash inducement, by most important performers. The brilliance of their concert grands unquestionably makes them the brand of choice for large halls. And Steinway still asks for and gets a 20 percent premium in price over any other American piano. By consensus, the only U.S.-made piano in its league is the Baldwin. Steinway's German pianos, produced in Hamburg, seem unchanged by cost-cutting "improvements" in Long Island City.

Equally unaffected by new ownership are two other great European pianos, the Bösendorfer and the Bechstein. Both are known for their warm, mellow tone and impeccable quality control in construction. Perfection has its price, though: figure $20,000 to $25,000 for a Bösendorfer, $15,000 to $20,000 for a Bechstein. The same size Steinway costs $8,000 to $10,000.

Hence, if money is no object and you don't intend to play Rachmaninoff at Carnegie Hall, buy a Bösendorfer or a Bechstein. A good alternative at one fourth to one half the price is a used prewar Steinway or Mason and Hamlin in excellent condition. The age of a used piano can be verified by comparing its serial number with listings in the Pierce Piano Atlas. Remember, however, that a used piano can be a risky investment unless you know something about piano construction or have reason to trust the dealer. Some instruments are lemons to begin with and never sound quite right. Others wear badly and may need expensive reconstruction long before their time.

For less money, say $3,000 to $6,000 for a medium grand, the choice is more difficult. Near the top of that range, new Baldwins provide good value and long guarantees. The best Japanese piano, the Yamaha, also has defenders: $4,000 buys an exceedingly sturdy instrument with a cool, brilliant tone. Yamahas have beautifully dressed cases, including a new shiny black finish that has it all over the standard ebonite. A third possibility would be a used prewar Knabe or Chickering. If they have been well cared for, the expensive components in pianos of this rank should last a lifetime or two. But the risks mount with pianos older than fifty or sixty years.

• THE BEST POISON
Just about anything ingested in sufficient quantity is poisonous—even Baskin-Robbins English Toffee, though the lethal dose is still unknown. People (and nature) have been hard at work perfecting toxic substances for a long time.

Old Favorites. Highly popular among the smart set in Renaissance Florence, arsenic has been widely used since the eighth century. As everyone knows, arsenic's extra dimension is its cumulative effect. While a single large dose of arsenic trioxide (white arsenic) can be fatal, few victims have succumbed in this fashion since the chemical is difficult to disguise, even in English cooking. But ingested over months, arsenic poisoning symptoms can be casually mistaken for degenerative natural causes.

Not so the other old reliable in the poisoner's pharmacopia. Strychnine (commonly used as rat poison) is quick and painful, producing unmistakable tetanus-like symptoms within minutes. It is extremely bitter—one part in a million can be tasted in solution—but the minute amount needed to kill made it the drug of choice for dozens of famous nineteenth-century murderers.

Equally celebrated and more common in sophisticated circles today, cyanide gas and salts have the advantage of producing death within seconds when taken in substantial doses. The pill Francis Gary Powers didn't swallow when he made his unscheduled stop in the USSR was potassium cyanide.

Unlike cyanide, another mystery writer's classic, belladonna, is a bit tamer than its reputation. Atropine, the active ingredient in belladonna (a.k.a. deadly nightshade) is a remarkably effective alkaloid poison. In small doses, however, atropine has numerous medical uses. Real danger comes from accidental consumption of deadly nightshade berries, which some kids can't resist sampling.

Accidental mushroom poisoning is, of course, much more common. *Amanita muscaria* figures prominently in the works of Dorothy L. Sayers and has a long, dishonorable history among real European royalty. It dries nicely, remaining potent for long periods in powdered form. But 90 percent of all mushroom poisonings worldwide come from eating the *Amanita phalloides*. *Phalloides* looks much like choice edible varieties and, from testimony, tastes scrumptious. Its toxin is slow-acting, causing distress only the next day. A bite or two is not fatal, but one good side dish will finish off your liver.

Animals. The world is absolutely teeming with poisonous insects, assorted reptiles, and fish. Luckily for us, they tend to leave Americans alone. An average of ten to twenty people die from snakebite each year in the United States; close to fifteen thousand succumb annually in India. Cobras, kraits, and Russell's vipers do most of the damage in Asia. In Latin America the fer-de-lance, palm viper, and bushmaster get in the most licks. Milligram per milligram, your deadliest land-snake venom comes from the Reevesby Island tiger snake; an Australian sea snake, the *Hydrophis belcheri,* is yet thirty times more potent.

Insects are overrated. Mosquitoes, flies, and lice do incredible damage spreading infection, but their bites aren't directly toxic. Tarantulas look just awful—big ones can reach seven or eight inches in length—but tarantula venom is not deadly. Only the female black widow spider can kill

an adult, and this occurs very infrequently. Still, black widow venom is no picnic, causing excruciating pain, muscle cramps, chills, and so forth.

More exotic killers include the stonefish (which looks

like a stone) found in the Pacific, the Australian box jelly-fish (which does not look like a box), and the gila monster. The latter, an otherwise peaceable inhabitant of the desert in the American Southwest, secretes a poison equal in stopping power to average rattlesnake venom.

Space Age Wonders. Where to begin. Among deliberate creations of science, chemical and biological warfare agents are highlights. Since peace-loving governments everywhere were not content with highly corrosive gases (notably phosgene, employed by both sides in World War I), a whole new array of poisons that can be absorbed through the skin and work directly on the nervous system has been developed. The most toxic nerve gas—at least, the most toxic anyone will talk about—is VX. Under ideal conditions, one pound of the stuff could kill a half million people.

Much less is known about the state of the art in biological poisons; the United States officially renounced both their development and their stockpiling several years ago. Since the general military purpose of biological weapons is to disable rather than kill, research was concentrated on non-fatal bacterial toxins. One incredibly successful strain, the *Pasteurella tularensis,* may rank ounce for ounce as the most effective poison ever deliberately manufactured for the purpose. In immeasurably minute concentrations, this organism causes rapid onset of a serious disease called tularemia, which is fatal about 5 percent of the time in young adults.

Our own candidate for the best poison is a dark horse, a relative newcomer on the scene. The element plutonium emits alpha particles, a particularly nasty, low-energy radioactive particle that causes cancer with devilish efficiency. Just how efficiently is a matter of controversy, but some experts believe that two billionths of a pound lodged in the lungs is likely to cause cancer over an ordinary lifetime. When polled, staff members at the Lawrence Nuclear Radiation Laboratory in California stated that they would not allow their children to play outdoors if the soil contained 1½ grams of plutonium *per square mile.*

At the moment, there is far less than that amount of plutonium outside bomb storage facilities. But give it time. Current federal energy program plans call for the use of plutonium as the basic fuel for generating electricity by the turn of the century. And once plutonium is created in nuclear reactor cores, it's kind of tough to get rid of—the stuff takes several hundred thousand years to decay.

• THE BEST POTATO CHIP

Whatever the virtues of modern technology, the powdered, reconstituted, flash-fried food module known as the Pringle New Fangled Potato Chip isn't one of them. That Procter and Gamble has managed to displace a good chunk of the chip market with its tennis-ball cans of molded carbohydrate is sobering evidence of cultural decline.

If you are one of the discerning few Americans who still consider the potato chip more than a vehicle for avocado dip, there's one way to strike back. Buy the ultimate chip— Kitch'n Cook'd. Kitch'n Cook'd chips hardly resemble standard brands, even the good ones like Wise; they are thicker, crunchier, and much tastier. The color of the Kitch'n Cook'd tends to deep brown, due to the high natural sugar content of the main raw ingredient, California russet potatoes. Ordinary chip manufacturers buy anemic, low-sugar Kennebec spuds on the theory that Americans prefer their junk food a uniform light tan. Also in their favor, Kitch'n Cook'd contain no preservative (other than salt) to sully the ambrosiac combination of vegetable oil and potato.

The source of all this goodness is the Maui Potato Chips Factory, Maui, Hawaii. Its owner, Dewey Kobayashi, has resisted the temptation to franchise Kitch'n Cook'd or sell out to the conglomerate god. Hence Kitch'n Cook'd are a scarce commodity. Few of Dewey's legendary chips leave the islands undigested, local demand exceeding supply. Tourists have been known to haul them home in suitcases by the carton, like vacationers returning from Curaçao with Seiko watches. About your only other shot at Kitch'n Cook'd is to win over Mr. Kobayashi by post. Most mail requests are turned down, but just in case, enclose a check for $6.30 plus postage.

 THE BEST RACEHORSE

First, forget about trotters. Trotters aren't racehorses. Neither are quarter horses, Arabians, or Appaloosas. We're talking about Thoroughbreds. Second, suspend disbelief; with over 20,000 Thoroughbreds foaled each year, and with some 250 vintages to choose among, we aren't going to get anywhere unless you have a little faith. Third, remember that no horse was ever best at everything. They just don't come with the competitiveness of Dr. Fager (who tried to bite any horse nervy enough to pass him), the stride of Secretariat ("like riding on a sofa," his jockey said, except this sofa covered twenty-five feet each time hoofs hit turf), the sheer muscle of Roseben (who once won carrying 147 pounds against rivals 60 pounds less encumbered), the sprinting ability of The Tretarch, and the prolificacy of Eclipse (from whom 90 percent of today's Thoroughbreds descend), all in one convenient 1,500-pound package.

Is it fair to compare today's racehorses with giants of the

past like Colin, Sceptre, St. Simon, or Man o' War, which raced over slower surfaces and made do without tetracycline and high-protein feed? Probably not. There's simply no telling whether Secretariat could have taken Man o' War, any more than we can ever know whether Joe Morgan could hit Walter Johnson's low, hard one.

But we do know that Thoroughbreds are bigger than ever and, on the average, can cover six furlongs in less time. Selective breeding's the key, of course. Winning hayburners end up on stud farms; the losers end up in Kal Kan.

Among recent American greats—European-bred horses are so inferior, French owners have begun lobbying to ban U.S. competition from the rich Continental races—consider the following candidates:

Bold Ruler. Triumphant victor of the 1957 Preakness and sire par excellence. Father of some eighty stakes winners, a success rate topped only by his daddy, Nasrullah.

Secretariat. Bold Ruler's most illustrious progeny. Took the Triple Crown without breathing hard, winning at Belmont by thirty-one lengths. He's already made a fortune at stud for his syndicate with much more to come; the first crop of good-looking colts sold for unheard-of prices.

Citation. The 1948 Triple Crown winner and, some nostalgia buffs insist, the track equal to Secretariat. Citation, alas, flunked miserably at stud.

Ruffian. The undefeated filly who set or tied a record every time she ran, only to stumble in a match race with Foolish Pleasure. Her death was front-page news in *The New York Times* and made grown sports editors weep.

Forego. Second celebrity (after Secretariat) of the 1970 All Stars, the best crop of colts ever foaled. A huge gelding; great weight carrier. Hauled 134 pounds for a mile and a half to win the 1975 Suburban Handicap; a year later, did it again, covering the last quarter mile of the Marlboro Cup in twenty-three seconds while toting 137 pounds around a muddy track.

Kelso. Five times Horse of the Year; all-time money winner ($1,977,896). Winner of the Woodward Stakes (four times), the Jockey Club Gold Cup (five times), the 1961 Handicap Triple Crown. A gelding, who on retirement was put to work chasing foxes, Mrs. Richard C. Du Pont in the saddle.

Dr. Fager. A dark horse, so to speak. Never really tested over long distances. A victim of dirty tricks: only beaten by Damascus when the opposition stable unleashed a "rabbit" to ruin the good doctor's pace. Still, Dr. Fager holds the record for the mile.

The best? None of the above. It's Native Dancer, the horse hardly anyone remembers to remember, probably because he blew the Derby. Yet what other Thoroughbred lost just one start of twenty-two, in races from five furlongs to a mile and a half? And what other Thoroughbred ever had the last word, even while losing? Native Dancer is the sire or grandsire of four Kentucky Derby winners.

• THE BEST REASON NOT TO GO TO COLLEGE

There are lots of good reasons to put in your four years behind the ivy—football weekends, late movies, coeducation, draft beer, squash. Even booklearning, which many believe sharpens the mind and soothes the spirit. But forget all that nonsense about making money. College is a dubious investment today, and there's every reason to believe it's getting worse.

Consider the numbers. Suppose you enter Vanderbilt in 1977. Tuition, room, and board will run over $5,000 a year to start, probably more like $7,000 by your senior year. Add on another $1,500 per year for books, cheeseburgers, Levi's, movies, and plane tickets, making a four-year total around $30,000. Next add the income you could have made during those years working without a sheepskin: conservatively figure $24,000 after taxes and net of room and board living at home, well below average factory earnings. For good measure, throw in the interest you could have kept on that $54,000 ($24,000 + $30,000) by socking it away in blue chips or utility bonds—say, $3,000 after taxes—which yields a grand total of $57,000.

That $57,000 nest egg, the alternative to a four-year sojourn in Nashville, represents the real cost of a first-class education. That $57,000 earns about $5,000 a year in safe investments, a difficult gap for a fresh college grad to make up without future expensive training. In fact, if our experienced blue-collar worker keeps banking his or her nest-egg income, the college grad may never catch up. At current returns, the $57,000 should double about every fourteen years. When our working stiff reaches thirty-five, the nest egg will have grown to $114,000; by age forty-nine, it will reach $228,000. So the blue-collar worker, simply by letting the hypothetical college nest egg plow back its proceeds, will have a pre-tax investment income of about $20,000 a year by late middle age. If you don't like these numbers, perhaps you'll take the word of an expert: Harvard economist Richard Freeman has calculated that the rate of return on a college education fell by about 30 percent from 1969 to 1973.

Of course, things could go wrong, leaving our high-school grad sorry he/she didn't go to college. Interest rates might fall; inflation might explode; prolonged unemployment might wipe out savings. But the future for college grads is equally uncertain. The wages of high-school graduates have risen sharply in relation to those of college graduates in the last six or seven years, and there's no reason to believe the trend won't continue. Once upon a time white-collar workers were almost immune to unemployment, but times are clearly different. Shuffling papers, it seems, is no longer a sure route to loot.

How could untold thousands of high-school guidance counselors be so wrong? Like many other things, it's a matter of supply and demand. First, more people want to go to college and more parents can afford to send them. In 1950, 20 percent of all older teenagers entered college; by 1976, the number was 45 percent, and the flood of graduates naturally tended to lower starting salaries. Also, blacks and women realized they were equally qualified to hold down cushier, high-prestige positions, and Congress agreed. With job discrimination slowly ebbing, the pool of would-be white-collar workers should grow steadily for quite a while longer.

Will boola-boola ever again be worth the investment? Probably not, since, given the opportunity, too many people would rather work behind a desk. Office wages will probably lag behind the pay for more arduous occupations, ultimately settling down to an uneasy balance.

• THE BEST REASON TO FOOL MOTHER NATURE

Sears, Roebuck's ad agency in the Northeast sent out a

memo before the 1975 Christmas rush cautioning radio and TV stations on the dangers of "editorializing" about the weather:

"The most common error made by most air personalities is that they tell people to stay home prior to the arrival of bad weather . . . It is a proven fact that people enjoy shopping in cold and inclement weather. Why not encourage their shopping rather than discouraging it? It's hard enough to create retail sales . . . We certainly don't need air personalities discouraging them."

The penalty for anti-capitalist pessimism: "If it becomes necessary that your station discourage driving we insist that all our spots scheduled during the period be canceled."

• THE BEST REASON TO PLAY FOOTBALL WITH A HELMET ON

"When I was very young, a Sunday School teacher told us that the beauty of Joseph's coat was its many colors. I'm not sure I understood the teacher's thought then, but I have since remembered it many times."   —Gerald R. Ford

• THE BEST REASON TO RIDE THE BUS

The state of New York has begun polling licensed drivers on how they want their remains disposed of, should they meet an unhappy end on a state highway.

We understand, however, that the bodies of other passengers may still be claimed by next of kin.

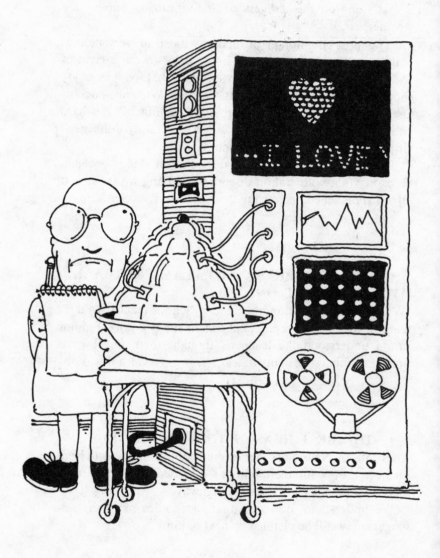

• THE BEST REASON TO STICK TO VANILLA CUSTARD

Dr. Adrian R. M. Upton, Associate Professor of Neurology at McMaster University, recently measured brain waves in a bowl of lime Jell-O. While Dr. Upton linked the brain-wave activity to natural errors in EEG machine readings, others believe the phenomenon is related to the lime's fierce will to live.

• THE BEST RESORT HOTEL IN THE UNITED STATES

Our cup runneth over. Is it the Breakers in Palm Beach, Henry Flagler's re-creation of Renaissance Italy decorated with Venetian glass, Flemish tapestries, and Park Avenue coupon-clippers? Or is it the Boca Raton Hotel down the coast, the resort that shares a beach with the richest city in America? Georgia's Cloister on Sea Island rates stars for civility, scenery, and tennis. And how can we pass by the Greenbrier (White Sulphur Springs, West Virginia) or the Homestead (Hot Springs, Virginia), mineral-water spas turned mountain retreats for the Eastern Establishment?

Colorado Spring's Broadmoor inspires fierce loyalty among the tennis/golf/fishing/ice skating crowd; Rancho Encantado, the carefully polished guest ranch outside Santa Fe, attracts the cream of desert fanciers. Along the California coast, there's the Biltmore in Santa Barbara, of course, not to mention the Del Monte Lodge in Pebble Beach.

Actually the best U.S. resort is to be found, not in North

America, but in Hawaii. Laurance Rockefeller built the 300-room Mauna Kea Beach Hotel in 1965 for $25 million. For his money Mr. Rockefeller got what might well be the perfect resort: a shimmering, low-slung structure with central gardens designed by Skidmore, Owings and Merrill, a mile of broad white beach on the isolated west coast of the Big Island, fifteen tennis courts, a 7,000-yard golf course.

Guests may scuba-dive or snorkel in undisturbed waters just beyond the breakers, stroll among 500 acres of palms and flowering gardens. On the championship Robert Trent Jones golf course, carved out of volcanic rock above the beach, players face one of the fifteen or twenty toughest rounds in the country, with long, broad fairways leading to small, heavily bunkered greens. Non-golfers can ward off ennui horseback riding or hunting wild boar on the 500-square-mile Parker Ranch, fishing by charter boat in Kaunoa Bay, or climbing the snow-capped Mauna Kea volcano.

Not surprisingly, the food is very good. American and muted European specialties: fresh fish, prime beef, Viennese pastry, whipped cream everywhere. Choose among three restaurants, including one on the terrace above the beach that serves a lunch buffet straight from the Gilded Age.

Unlike most plush hotels, the detail here is as fine as the conception. Public rooms are decorated with primitive art from the South Pacific and southern Asia. Breakfast tables have individual toasters, so you get your english muffins the way you want them. A staff perhaps 50 percent larger than necessary keeps the grounds absolutely spotless, polishes the brass fixtures daily, leaves an orchid blossom on your pillow each evening.

Perfection, as might be expected, is not a bargain. Built

by a millionaire, the hotel caters to millionaires, or at the very least those who fake it pretty well. Rooms for two with breakfast and dinner run about $125. What with a crack at the wild game, that buffet lunch, and a bottle of Château Haut-Brion at dinner, even a Rockefeller might feel the pinch.

• THE BEST ROLLER COASTER

Much controversy here, based on misunderstandings about what makes roller coasters—ah—roller coasters. The *Guinness Book of World Records* lists the 110-foot-high Racer in Chapultepec Park, Mexico City, as the world's highest. *Guinness* won't even hazard a guess on the fastest, though we would accept the unauthenticated claim of Six Flags Over Mid-America Park near St. Louis for its new 62 mph Screamin' Eagle.

Actually it takes more than height and speed to make a good ride. Suspense and fear are the crucial ingredients, the former an underrated virtue. Suspense is typically achieved by increasing the time it takes to reach the first summit, the train barely inching forward, cogs grinding ominously. But suspense also depends on subtler design points—hiding the

drop from view until the last split second, shielding waiting patrons from a good look at the track layout, yet permitting screams to filter back from distant cars. Speed doesn't make a roller coaster frightening, it's acceleration: free-fall drops, absolute weightlessness at the peaks, gut-wrenching turns with no chance for anticipation. Disorientation helps, too. That's why the second ride is never as good as the first.

Among the greats, many experts swear by Coney Island's old-timer the Cyclone. This is because too many experts grew up in New York, not benefiting from the consciousness-expanding experience of the Blue Streak of Cedar Point Amusement Land (Sandusky, Ohio, fifty miles west of Cleveland) or the Cyclone—no relation—in Lakeside Amusement Park, Denver. A newer, absolutely first-rate example of the classic roller coaster is the Great American Scream Machine at the Six Flags Over Georgia Park in Atlanta.

Three attempts to improve on the classic (with mixed success) should also be noted. The first two, Kings Island (Cincinnati) and Kings Dominion (Richmond) sport identical Racers—long, fast rides with twin tracks. The gimmick: two trains leave the gate simultaneously, taking separate routes, then racing to the finish. The verdict: only A—. Slick and exhilarating, but not frightening. An older Racer utilizing the same idea can be found at Kennywood near Pittsburgh.

The world's most expensive roller coaster, Walt Disney World's $17 million Space Mountain, is another animal altogether. Space Mountain is completely enclosed in a twenty-story-high, blacked-out dome. The combination of high g-turns and no possible visual fix makes for one of the most terrifying rides east of the Santa Monica Freeway.

For sheer thrills, though, nobody can beat the Thunderbolt at the aforementioned Kennywood Park in Pittsburgh. One of the four (yes, four!) big-league coasters at Kennywood, Thunderbolt is built into the side of a bluff overlooking the Monongahela River 300 feet below. Its two major drops go directly over the cliff with rescue from instant death a near thing. Fear is honed by some really brutal turns over tracks that, on inspection, appear to be much too old to tolerate the abuse. And just when you are sure the worst is over, the Thunderbolt takes one last suicidal plunge before heading back home. Merits a detour.

 THE BEST SCOTCH

Sample the habits of the upper-middle-income, mortgage-bearing. Volvo-driving, two-weeks-every-winter-in-Antigua crowd, and you will find that scotch is no longer the drink of choice. The *de rigeur* Dewars and water before business lunch has been replaced by the anonymous Bloody Mary, Bullshot, or Noilly Prat on the rocks; at special occasions, Chivas must now compete with iced Polish vodka.

Many mourn the passing of the true status whiskey—mourners include distillers and speculators who are stuck with inventories that will take a decade to wipe out. We do not. Fame and fortune have taken their toll on scotch, changing its flavor as well as its image.

Ninety-nine percent of all scotches in the United States are blends, mixtures of dozens of whiskeys layered on a

BONNIE BRAE'S BAR AND GRILLE

base of tasteless grain alcohol. No one knows exactly why the hundred or so distillers produce such distinctively flavored brews. The raw ingredients—common barley and yeast—are not special. They're not even grown in Scotland. The deep, wood-like taste varies with the length of time the malted barley is exposed to peat smoke while it dries, but this touch of smoke in unblended scotch does not explain subtle differences between distilleries. Color variations are determined by the type of oak cask employed for aging, which in any case has virtually no effect on flavor.

Experts, for want of a better explanation, concentrate on the water used and the shape of the stills. Obsolete nineteenth-century equipment is endlessly repaired for fear that a new piece of copper tubing, a slight permutation in technique, will queer the works.

Variations among brand-name scotches depend upon age and blend. Old scotch mellows without losing taste, though most connoisseurs doubt whiskey can improve beyond twelve years in the cask. Blending is more important, with each standard brand using a secret recipe to achieve the expected taste. Flavorful Highland malts have less body than typical Islay and Campbeltown malts; Lowland malts are relatively weak on flavor and body.

But efforts to expand the market and cut costs have narrowed the gaps between extremes in blends, say between Ballantine and Cutty Sark. While we have no proof to offer, there's reason to believe that nearly all brands contain more neutral grain spirits—read vodka—than ever before. Less bite for less money. The Scots themselves claim not to be able to tell the difference between popular brands. Just try picking out your own favorite in a blindfold test.

Thus all the really fine scotches must be tasted unblended as single malt whiskies from single distilleries. A few are available in the United States: light-bodied, heavily flavored Glenfarclas, incredibly smoky Laphroaig. Yet none compares with the more balanced Glenlivet from the distillery of George and J. G. Smith. Glenlivet costs about as much as premium twelve-year-old blends containing Glenlivet, like Haig and Haig Pinch, and Johnnie Walker Black Label. Sip it the way you would cognac, undiluted at room temperature. Or drink it the way the Scots do: plain, with just a few drops of spring water to improve the bouquet.

• THE BEST SENATOR

There is no objective standard of excellence for politicians. After all, one person's stroganoff may be another's Alpo. Instead of a single entree, we offer a full menu:

The Most Liberal. The Senate is full of liberals only too glad to appear at ADA fund-raisers or denounce malnutrition in their monthly newsletters. The number who will defend unpopular liberal causes, like busing and the abolition of capital punishment, or stand up to lobbyists from the aerospace, oil, gun, banking, and textile industries, is much smaller. Of course, in some cases a liberal stance would mean instant political death. George McGovern (South Dakota) can hardly be blamed for opposing handgun licensing; Dick Clark (Iowa) must mind his P(arity)'s and Q(uota)'s on farm issues.

By most standards Ribicoff, Bayh, Kennedy, Proxmire, and Nelson do pretty well. Our choice, though, is Frank Church, a Democrat from Republican Idaho. Church has been a liberal activist in the Senate since his election twenty years ago, recently making a splash as the head of the Select Committee on Intelligence Operations. What separates Church from the liberal pack, however, is his early attack on LBJ's Vietnam policy, a stance not likely to have helped the senator either at home or in Washington.

The Most Conservative. Conservatism is very trendy, which makes the Senate a very trendy place these days. Some conservative ideologues quite naturally face problems similar to those of their liberal colleagues. When push comes to shove, few are willing to sacrifice careers in defense of Fiscal Responsibility or the freedom-loving peoples of Taiwan. However, the number of safe seats from the South and West give an unusually large proportion of

Senate conservatives the opportunity to vote as they please, which leaves us with too many candidates.

Carl Curtis, James McClure, Jake Garn, and Dewey Bartlett fit the conservative mold without a wrinkle, none ever betraying a hint of sympathy for welfare mamas, un-employed black teen-agers, Cambridge intellectuals, or liberated women. All are disqualified, though, on the grounds that no one, including their constituents, has ever heard of them.

Among better-known senators, James Eastland and John Stennis do very nicely on roll-call votes, but one has the feeling these Deep South grandees are performing by reflex alone. For that matter, Barry Goldwater may still believe that extremism in the pursuit of liberty is no vice, but rumor has it he's turned soft on Nelson Rockefeller and détente.

Hence our choice, the least soft of conservatives, Strom Thurmond. Not merely is the Republican (ex-Dixiecrat) from South Carolina on the record against busing, handgun control, boycotting Rhodesian exports, and reductions in overseas troops, while in favor of no-knock searches, capital punishment, segregation, filibusters, textile import quotas, and the B-1 bomber. Thurmond manages to defend his views with a zeal seldom found in this exclusive old men's club, and once even topped off a debate with Texas liberal Ralph Yarborough with a public fistfight.

The Richest. Skeptics might wonder what personal wealth has to do with being the best senator. Don't ask us, ask the electorate. In their infinite wisdom, American voters have chosen to populate the Senate with more millionaires per capita than the Knickerbocker Club.

Probably the richest senator of our time was Robert Kerr of Oklahoma, who died in 1963 owning $40 million worth of Kerr-McGee Oil. Kerr, incidentally, was not shy about his source of livelihood, using his chairmanship of the Senate Finance Committee to protect the energy industry from unpatriotic encroachments on the oil depletion allowance. Choosing among the recent crop isn't so easy, however, since they tend to keep low profiles.

Lowell Weicker (Squibb Drug), Barry Goldwater (department stores), Edward Kennedy (rum, real estate), Charles Percy (Bell and Howell), James Buckley (oil, broadcasting), Harry Byrd, Jr. (apple orchards, newspapers), Lloyd Bentsen (agriculture, corporate law), and Hiram Fong (farming, insurance, construction) could all manage to make ends meet without their salaries. Our hunch, though, for senator with the wolf farthest from the door is James Eastland.

Eastland grows cotton in Sunflower County, Mississippi. Just how much cotton we can't say for sure. But we do know that the second-ranking member of the Senate Agriculture Committee receives an average of $150,000 annually from federal cotton subsidy programs.

The Most Powerful. Once upon a time, power in the United States Senate was a matter of seniority. The chairmen of the great committees—Finance, Armed Services, Agriculture, Appropriations, Foreign Relations, Judiciary, Banking—controlled the fate of important legislation. All you had to do to become a chairman was to get re-elected four or five times and avoid acute alcoholic brain syndrome. Southern politicians like Georgia's Richard Russell dominated the Congress through a combination of oligarchical leadership at home, administrative skill in the hearing room, and preservation of the filibuster.

Chairpeople still exercise a lot of power, but no longer can they count on years of service as a substitute for slick logrolling inside the club. The threat of internal uprising against the seniority system is too credible to risk defiance of the committee majority. Even when there is no question of removing chairpeople, lesser mortals are more likely to find a way around their wishes. West Virginia's Jennings Randolph, for example, found himself on the losing end of a confrontation with Ed Muskie over the diversion of federal highway funds for mass transit.

Among Republicans, Clifford Case, Charles Percy, and Jacob Javits work hard and effectively, yet are viewed with suspicion by their rural and Sun-Belt confreres. Thurmond, Tower, and Goldwater use seniority relatively well, but have a limited hard-line constituency. As a practical matter, Howard Baker could come closest to real power if the Republicans were ever able to gain control of Congress, or at least free themselves from subservience to the White House.

Democrats with clout come in two versions. The first variety is the senator with a national constituency, support from traditional party allies (labor, civil rights), or an independent grass-roots power base. It also helps to have a safe seat, so that the home front provides as little distraction as possible from the business of moving and shaking. Muskie, Humphrey, Kennedy, and Jackson all qualify easily. McGovern does not, but his exceptional ability to draw press coverage makes him a member of the elite.

The second group is made up of insiders, senators whose power comes from seniority or less formal leadership positions within Congress. Of course, the two groups overlap— Muskie controls billions of dollars of federal pollution grants, Jackson uses committee positions to influence environmental and defense legislation. But some insiders are practically invisible to the public. California's Alan Cranston knows how to trade small talk and favors to best advantage when need be; his liberal friends would have liked to make him majority leader when Mansfield retired. John McClellan (Arkansas), Herman Talmadge (Georgia), John Stennis (Mississippi), and Warren Magnuson (Washington) play the seniority game perfectly, never irritating their peers unnecessarily, never violating the unwritten rules. In the same group, Russell Long (Louisiana) deserves special mention, using his chair on the Finance Committee to control tax legislation and take good care of his friends in the energy industry.

Our own candidate: Robert Byrd of West Virginia, the man who took the majority whip away from Ted Kennedy in 1971 and the majority leadership away from Hubert Humphrey in 1977. Byrd has brought a number of advantages to both jobs. He owes nothing to special interests back home, he is incredibly hardworking, his politics offend neither right nor left—at least, not very much. Perhaps most important, though, his uncharismatic demeanor makes him a poor prospect for national office, rendering him a harmless ally for ambitious peers. Other senators may reform taxes, save us from foreign entanglements, or plan for national health insurance, but, on any given day, it is Byrd who is most likely to show up with the votes in his pocket.

• THE BEST SOAP OPERA

Can Julie Horton find happiness wed to Doug Williams, her widowed stepfather? What secret about Doug's past clouds Julie's life as well as that of Julie's stepsister (Doug's daughter), Hope Williams, and the entire Horton clan?*

* See note on page 140.

137

You may not care, but 8 million regular viewers of "Days of Our Lives" (1:30–2:30, 12:30 Central Time) do, not to mention head writer Patricia Falken-Smith, who makes $300,000 a year snipping loose plot ends, actors Susan and Bill Hayes, who together earn $150,000 playing Julie and Doug, and the NBC executives, who figure the show banks an annual profit of $20 million.

Soap-opera fans are supposed to be housewives. Lately,

however, closet addicts from every shuffle of life have been confessing their devotion: "All My Children" and "The Young and the Restless" empty classrooms on many a campus. "Mary Hartman, Mary Hartman" is supposed to be a spoof on the soaps; in truth, wisps of satire are offered only to save face for an audience that would never admit to watching "Another World" or "One Life to Live."

No *Best* entry has proved more difficult to research. One assistant became hopelessly hooked on "General Hospital" and, after going cold turkey for three weeks, still wakes up in the middle of the night wondering how Marcia Weber would cope with the return of her lover Rick from an African prison after Marcia had given up hope and married Rick's younger brother, Jeff. Another brave volunteer went through three pounds of pecan sandies before mastering the story line of "Search for Tomorrow." Our nominations:

Best Plot. How can you beat "All My Children," which pits a son's love of his mom against a man's love for his helpmate?

Best Scandal. Bigamy tears apart the lives of Arlene Lovell and her husband (?) Ben Harper on "Love of Life." With Ben in jail for the aforementioned crime, Arlene accepts ill-gotten gains from underworld heavy Ray Slater to pay her mother's hospital bills.

Most Modern. In "Ryan's Hope," liberated woman attorney Jill Coleridge fights to save Dr. Seneca Beaulac from a murder conviction, after Dr. Beaulac confesses to shutting off his terminally sick wife's respirator. The case helps take Jill's mind off her star-crossed love for Catholic ward heeler Frank Ryan.

Oldest But Goodest. "The Guiding Light" celebrates its fortieth year on the air as Joe Werner faces the heartbreak of angina pectoris, Mike Bauer squares off against bigamist Spence Jeffers, Barbara Norris attempts to win the love of stepson Roger, Ed Bauer learns to accept the fact that his daughter Christina was actually fathered by another, and Leslie Bauer is killed by a hit-and-run driver who happens to be Leslie's husband's enemy, Spence Jeffers.

*Doug was never legally married to Addie, Julie's and Hope's mother. It was an honest mistake—unknown to him, Doug's divorce from Kim, his previous wife, was held up on a technicality. This will be cold comfort for Hope, however, if the news gets out; illegitimacy is not taken lightly in Salem, her home town. Kim's employer, lawyer Don Craig, contemplates spilling the beans since he is in love with Julie. Doug's best shot may be a quick divorce from Kim, once Kim has settled the problem of the property in Polynesia that she and Doug have inherited from Kim's parents. One complication: Don and Kim know that Doug, under the name of Brent Douglas, was once imprisoned for stock fraud, a fact he has successfully hidden from Julie, Hope, and the Salem bourgeoisie.

• THE BEST SOLUTION TO THE ENERGY CRISIS

Unpleasant Fact No. 1: The Sheiks have us over a barrel.

When OPEC tripled crude-oil prices after the 1973 embargo, the age of cheap gas probably ended forever. Not because the world is running out of oil—there's enough left to last for two hundred years, give or take fifty. But because the cheap sources are concentrated in a few Mideast sandpiles. Saudi Arabia could deliver petroleum to tankers in the Persian Gulf for fifty cents a barrel. They charge twelve dollars and will continue to get away with it because new oil from the North Sea or Alaska or aging Texas wells costs almost that much to get to market.

Prospects for breaking the oil cartel are dim. The OPEC nations know they'll never get stuck with their reserves; it's a matter of how much to sell now and how much later. The very largest producers—Saudi Arabia and Kuwait, for example—are swimming in oil revenues. Only Iran, Algeria, Venezuela, and Indonesia need cash badly enough to risk cheating on the cartel, and they pump just a modest fraction of total world demand. Besides, Iran is a vigorous supporter of OPEC, privately arguing for higher prices to quench its thirst for foreign currency.

Unpleasant Fact No. 2: The North Slope won't save us.

Each year American wells produce less, leaving us increasingly at the mercy of Colonel Qaddafi. Exploitation of the North Slope of Alaska, East Coast offshore deposits, and low-potential domestic reserves could, in theory, make us self-sufficient in oil for fifty years. Theory doesn't mean much, however. This additional oil would be very expensive—perhaps more than twenty dollars a barrel—and the oil companies don't fancy making the investment without guaranteed profits. What's good for the country isn't necessarily good for Exxon.

Unpleasant Fact No. 3: Synthetic fuels won't save us.

Engineers can extract liquid fuels from almost anything these days: shale rock, tar sands, coal, sawdust, even cow pies. Colorado alone has larger energy reserves (locked up in shale) than Saudi Arabia. The trouble is, these synthetic fuels make Arab crude look like a bargain. Current estimates for coal liquidification run twenty-six dollars per barrel; shale oil may be a little cheaper, though the cost of getting rid of rock wastes and cleaning up polluted water probably eliminates that edge. Perhaps in the long run we'll figure out a practical synthetic to replace petroleum, or perhaps we'll all drive go-karts.

Unpleasant Fact No. 4: Coal and nuclear power are bad for children and other living things.

The first step to self-sufficiency is to stop using oil or natural gas to make electricity. American coal (one third the coal in the world) could produce all the raw power needed for 500 years. What's more, it's much cheaper than oil and output could be expanded rapidly by strip-mining surface deposits in the Western states. The catch is that coal is the dirtiest of fuels, spewing fine, cancer-causing ash and sulphur dioxide gas as it burns. This doesn't mean that coal can't or shouldn't be substituted for foreign oil. If we do switch, though, we'll pay a price in pollution.

Nuclear power is something else. When it works, it works fine. Less muss, less fuss—just as the ads promise. Yet no one has figured out what to do with the mountain of spent radioactive fuel we'll be forced to collect and isolate for hundreds of thousands of years. A second problem: the scarcity of uranium will make it necessary to "breed" plutonium fuel in reactors. Plutonium is the single most lethal substance known (see "Best Poison"), as well as being a convenient material from which to fashion homemade nuclear bombs.

Unpleasant Fact No. 5: Safe, plentiful energy is coming, but don't hold your breath.

Scientists have all sorts of good ideas about energy nirvana. First there's nuclear fusion, the power source of the hydrogen bomb. Russian, British, and U.S. experimenters are virtually certain that controlled fusion will be practicable. Then there's solar energy—home heating units, direct conversion of sunlight to electricity, giant solar-energy-collecting satellites that would send power to earth via microwaves. Wind and ocean-wave motion may be converted to electricity by means of newly designed generators; prototypes are already in use.

The problem is money and time. Even simple solar water heaters won't be produced in sufficient quantity to make a dent for another ten years. In a better world, the price of clean, convenient fuels like natural gas and oil would have increased by 10 or 15 percent each year, starting sometime in the 1950's: fast enough to encourage research on substitutes, yet slow enough to allow for smooth adjustment. But then, in a better world, rain wouldn't fall on weekends and hot fudge sundaes wouldn't have calories.

Moral: Save a watt.

Every "easy" solution to the energy crisis, from nuclear breeder reactors, to offshore oil wells, to synthetic fuels, is either unconscionably dangerous or unconscionably expensive. The sensible solution is figuring out how to make do with less. Energy conservation doesn't mean a return to horse and buggies. Western Europeans and Japanese seem to manage nicely on half the electricity and gasoline.

Of course, we can always rely on the goodwill of Colonel Qaddafi . . .

• **THE BEST STAND-IN FOR DORIAN GRAY**
The halls of the Justice Department in Washington are rich with the likenesses of former Attorneys General, it being a policy to commission portraits as they retire. The latest to be so honored is Richard Kleindienst, who pleaded guilty in

federal court in 1974 to the charge of telling far less than the whole truth to a Senate committee.

Plans for the unveiling of John Mitchell's portrait have not been announced.

• THE BEST STOCKBROKER

A subject of no small interest among the movers and shakers who populate the southern tip of Manhattan by day. The securities industry takes the brokering trade very seriously, and well it might. Hot brokerage houses reap millions annually from mutual funds, insurance companies, pension funds, bank trust departments, and other big customers searching for ways to beat the odds. Many a Park Avenue co-op and Mercedes 450 SLC has been financed by correctly predicting the fortunes of high-flyers like Polaroid or LTV. Your average $14,000-a-year B.A. from USC can become a $180,000-a-year research department genius on the strength of one big find, one Haloid Corporation, or even a Schlumberger.

Regrettably, the stock-market-advice business is 49 percent con and 49 percent self-delusion. The evidence is overwhelming that no person (or computer) can predict the future price of a stock from the history of its past price. Successful "technical" analysts are just luckier than the rest of us or, like fortune tellers, have mastered the art of hedging ("The Dow Jones will reach 1,100 by May, unless the market develops a triple top and bottom pattern late this winter").

Fundamental analysis, predicting future stock prices from long-term earnings prospects, works better, but so many people have access to the same information that stock prices typically adjust to hard news within hours. Inside information? Forget it. The Securities and Exchange Commission frowns—no, scowls—at the use of privileged info to make a buck. Anyone who takes the risk of getting rich this way isn't going to advertise the fact in Uncle Hermie's broker's newsletter.

Where does this leave you? On your own. The best stockbroker is the one who follows instructions and asks for the smallest commission in return. Since all the brokers we know follow instructions pretty well, picking the best comes down to picking the cheapest.

Until May 1975 all brokers had identical commission schedules, set by the stock exchanges. Large trades subsi-

dized small trades, since the actual cost of buying and selling wasn't much different whether 200 or 2,000 shares changed hands. With the end of fixed commissions, competition has pushed down the price for high-volume transactions by 70 to 80 percent, but actually raised the price charged on $2,000 to $10,000 sales by brand-name brokerage firms.

However, if you are willing to forgo some amenities—chitchat with a customers' person, a comfortable seat from which to view the ticker in person—a number of discount brokers will trade in your name for about two thirds or less the old rates. Discounters rarely offer research reports and have no opinions to peddle. Some insist that you spend a modest minimum amount each year on your account. All are insured by the same agency that makes good when any brokerage house goes bankrupt.

The cheapest we've run into is Stock Cross (141 Milk Street, Boston, Massachusetts 02109, 617-482-8200). For example, it will sell 200 shares of Southern Company at 15 for a $42 commission (versus $74 at Merrill Lynch), 300 shares of Mid Continent Telephone at 14 for $50.50 (versus $93 at Merrill Lynch). Prices are based only on the number of shares bought or sold; there is no minimum purchase required per year. At least two New York brokers, Source Securities Corp. (70 Pine Street, 800-221-2430) and Quick and Rielly (25 Broadway, 212-363-8686), offer comparable rates on small trades. In Chicago, try Burke, Christensen and Lewis (313-346-8283); San Francisco: Charles Schwab and Co. (415-398-1500).

If you still prefer your broker with turban and crystal ball, we offer one other recommendation. Customers' representative Anthony Silverman of Minneapolis buys and sells for his own account on the advice of his pedigreed golden retriever, Sumner of Kenwood. Mr. Silverman spreads out the New York Stock Exchange listings on the carpet, coaxing the dog to lie down on them. Silverman then buys the stock closest to researcher Sumner's first nail on her right paw.

T

THE BEST TRAVELER'S CHECKS

"American Express Traveler's Checks: Don't leave home without them," Karl Malden sagely advises. Millions obey. Arthur Frommer's pitch for Barclays is less authoritarian: of course you're going to carry traveler's checks, he reasons, but why pay for butter when the low-priced spread tastes the same?

Traveler's checks, as is obvious to all who witness American Express's object lessons on prime-time TV, are big business. No one makes money selling checks; the name of the game is "float." Since the average purchaser holds checks uncashed for a month or two, the issuing banks and finance companies can keep billions of your money invested at all times—two to three billions, to be precise. At 7 or 8 percent, interest on the "float" may reach $200 million a year.

Which brand to buy depends upon what's important to you:

Safety. All checks are safe in the sense that you'll eventually get your money back if you lose them. But some claims are processed in one hour, some in one year; and time may mean the difference between inconvenience and a busted vacation. No company will provide a quick refund without the check receipt and personal identification.

American Express has the fewest claim offices among the major issuers—in most places, claimants must find an Amex travel branch—but provides $100 emergency refunds at Holiday Inns in the United States and Avis booths everywhere else. This service can be very important if you lose your wad at 5 p.m. on Friday afternoon. Bank of America prides itself on what comes closest to a full instant refund. Just present your receipt at one of 28,000 correspondent banks and swear you aren't committing fraud. Cook's, Barclays, and New York's Citibank all pay out enough to get you through the crisis, then make a full refund within a few days as long as you don't ring bells on the Interpol Teletype. Finding a refund agent is easy for any of the majors, but can be a problem if you carry checks from the Third National Bank and Lawn Care Service of Missoula.

Acceptability. American Express wraps up more than half of the traveler's checks market, worldwide. So, chances are, more merchants, hotels, and banks in any given city have seen Amex checks before and understand that they aren't just play money. This does not mean, however, that American Express checks are accepted in more places. Check issuers are not legally obligated to redeem their own checks if they think the signatures are forged, so merchants take a risk when they take your paper. Ironically, the risk is smaller with checks other than American Express, since the smaller companies don't dare spoil the market for their product by refusing to honor a suspicious signature. Thus, while in practice all major checks are easy to cash, Cook's, Citibank, Barclays, and B. of A. may be a little easier.

A postscript: during days or weeks of international

financial upheaval, foreign banks may refuse checks in certain currencies. Problems are bigger for the British pound and Italian lira, but in the past decade the dollar hasn't been so almighty either. If things look shaky when you are about to embark, consider the option of buying checks in

German marks or Swiss francs. They cost extra, since you end up exchanging currencies one extra time, but they could be worth it.

Price. Different banks charge different amounts for the same brand of check. The only certainty is that American Express will cost as much or more than any other—1 percent of the face value, rounded up to the nearest dollar. Barclays checks are service-charge-free at Barclays branches and, as of this writing, at about two thirds of the assorted banks and S & L's that issue them. Bank of America has been known to offer package deals in which traveler's checks are thrown in free if you maintain a checking account. Thomas Cook & Sons issues its own checks free at its main New York office, but allows banks to charge for the service, if they choose. And last but not least, Citibank has a sale each May, permitting purchases up to $5,000 for just a $2 fee. This ploy is particularly clever, since Citibank entices summer vacationers to buy checks early, thereby letting the bank collect interest on the float that much longer.

U THE BEST UNDISCOVERED FRENCH RESTAURANT IN NEW YORK

Our needs are simple: nice, juicy lamb, *pommes gratinées*, a young Côtes du Rhône, romaine with a decent vinaigrette, enough elbow room to relax, a check under fifteen dollars per person.

Many restaurants in New York fit this description, at

least for a few months after they open. Then they are felled by a virus that seems to be triggered by Friday reviews in *The New York Times*. Stars (at least two, sometimes three) are bestowed. Reservations are made Tuesday morning for Saturday evening. Come Saturday, dinner is preceded by a forty-minute wait at the tiny bar, owing to unanticipated congestion in the kitchen. The lamb is juicy, but not pink; the potatoes lack parmesan. Regrettably the cellar is temporarily out of the Côtes du Rhône, but a 1973 Mouton Cadet is produced to be drunk over the last of the lamb. The waiter is harried, but friendly.

Weeks later, signs of recovery. Same crowd at the door, but five dollars to the maître d'hôtel solves the problem. Côtes du Rhône has been restored, though the chef seems to have permanently forgotten that rack of lamb should be served pink. Salade is now à la carte; for that matter, so is everything else, including the broiled-tomato garnish. The bill comes to fifty-eight dollars, although that does include six dollars for two dry vermouths at the bar.

Few New York French restaurants seem totally immune to success disease, which leaves strategists with two choices. The conservative approach is to stick with mature establishments that have built up resistance to the bug from a relatively mild attack during infancy. Among moderate-priced restaurants, Le-Bec-Fin and two West Side French ghetto bistros, Pierre au Tunnel and Du Midi, certainly qualify. For more money there's the Périgord Park, Chez Pascal, or Residence. Périgord Park, in particular, has survived an early bout of heavy tippers from Teaneck. At the top of the heap, few can complain of abuse from the two traditional quenelles palaces, La Caravelle and Lutèce.

For the adventurous, the alternative is to try anything that looks promising and take pleasure from a few good meals until *New York* magazine shows up. The trick here is to recognize sure losers before they have a shot at your American Express card. Regard with suspicion any Manhattan restaurant that (a) has an Art Deco interior, (b) calls itself French-Continental, French-Italian, or French-anything else, (c) has more than fifteen entrées on the menu, (d) has a French menu with English translations, or (e) lists expensive wines without vintage years. Do not enter any Manhattan restaurant that (a) advertises in the *Post,* (b) sports a *Cue* decal in the window, (c) offers free two-hour parking, or (d) has food photographs on the menu.

With no particular reason to believe that our current find will remain undiscovered until press time, we suggest a trip to La Mangeoire (Second Avenue and Fifty-third). It's a rather large place—hardly an auspicious sign—but the heavy use of potted plants and staggered room levels gives it an intimate feeling. The menu does not overreach; sauces that would require split-second timing are absent. Try the heavily garlicked *saucisse* with potatoes or the cold marinated mushrooms to begin, the filet of sole or rack of lamb for two as an entrée. Where appropriate, La Mangeoire serves genuine, thin-cut french fries, hot from the fat and tasting faintly of grated cheese. As in most bourgeois French restaurants, the desserts are relatively weak. Sample profiteroles (A+ chocolate sauce), house chocolate cake, or fresh fruit salad.

The wine list has to be one of the nicest in its class. Bordeaux were obviously purchased since the bottom fell out of the wine market, and the management isn't greedy about mark-ups. Everything is three or four dollars above store prices.

Lunch, with a half bottle of wine, averages nine dollars

per person. A big dinner with suitable alcoholic refreshment runs twelve to twenty dollars.

• THE BEST UNDISCOVERED HOTEL IN LONDON

Forsake the eighty-dollars-a-night swank of Mayfair and the huge, impersonal commercial establishments spread around Regents Park, Marylebone, St. James, and the Strand. London still has at least one well-located hotel of modest size and substantial comfort that's not too pricy.

It's the Basil Street (8 Basil Street) in Knightsbridge (S.W.3), a hundred yards south of Hyde Park and within walking distance of Buckingham Palace, Piccadilly, and the shops of Kensington. With just 123 rooms, fine service, and elegant Regency period pieces in the public rooms, the Basil could pass for a private club. No brush-offs from the bell captain, no Swedish tour groups lining up for 6 a.m. inspection in the corridors. Your room may not be oversized, and the bathrooms are certainly showing their age, but these drawbacks are more than offset by the charms of British service and British calm. Figure twenty-five dollars for a single, thirty-five to forty-five dollars for a double, at 1976 exchange and inflation rates.

The Basil has a dining room that preserves the club image: English roasts and grills, a decent wine card, unobtrusive service. But resist the temptation, if you can, since one of the best restaurants in London is just a block away: the Capitol Hotel at 22 Basil Street offers a rack of lamb that rivals the best of France.

V THE BEST VEHICLE IN WHICH TO PASS THROUGH THE EYE OF A NEEDLE

Many religious leaders renounce material possessions, but the Reverend Sun Myung Moon of the Unification Church is not in the position to make this sacrifice. "Christians think that the Messiah must be poor and miserable. He did not come for this," confides a manual published by the Unification Church. "Messiah must be the richest . . ."

All God's creations, alive or anthropomorphized, apparently yearn to belong to the Reverend Moon, the green bills in other people's pockets "crying" to be liberated. Even the lowly products of Detroit's production lines brazenly seek a place in His tent: the Reverend Moon's limousine arrived by itself "with a speed of 200 miles per hour and said, if Father didn't receive it, it would kill him."

W THE BEST WAY TO END THE BICENTENNIAL

The Jacwil Casket Company of Knightstown, Indiana, has created a special "Spirit of '76" model, colorfully decorated in red, white, and blue. Just the thing for those who care enough to end the very best.

• THE BEST WAY TO MAKE A SAFE CIGARETTE

R. J. Reynolds' Now cigarettes contain only 2 mg tar and 0.2 mg nicotine. They also contain one third less tobacco than run-of-the-mill smokes.

• THE BEST WAY TO SKIN A CAT

Or an elephant or a whale. Just leave it to a colony of common dermestid beetles, which are happy to eat anything organic that comes their way. Many large museums keep a

colony on retainer in the basement, offering the hungry bugs a fresh treat when the situation demands. Nature's way of getting down to the bone turns out to be much more practical than chemicals or mechanical means, particularly for delicate specimens.

Of course, the dermestid's eclectic tastes limit their value if all you want to remove is the animal's skin. Dermestid larvae, initiated at birth into the clean-plate club, eat everything down to the bone, and have even been known to polish off a wooden floor board or two for dessert.

• THE BEST WAY TO SPEND A NIGHT IN PHILADELPHIA

If you think W. C. Fields had the last word on this subject, the joke's on you. Sure, Philly isn't London or Rome, but the City of Brotherly Love has more going for it than Frank Rizzo and fried scrapple.

Hotels. Skip the convention palaces and try the traditional Barclay on Rittenhouse Square, or the smaller Latham, with its 150 rooms all done up in Italian provincial.

Restaurants. Don't worry about mixing up Old Original Bookbinders and Bookbinder's Sea Food House: they're both overpriced and overpraised. Philadelphia's real seafood house is called The Fish Market. Two restaurants, La Panetière and Le Bec Fin, take the idea of haute cuisine seriously; the smaller Bec Fin succeeds with more consistency. Less ambitious French food at less ambitious prix can be had at the Garden or Le Bistro. Everybody's first choice for fettucini is Gaetano's, the only place around with homemade pasta. Less well known to non-Philadelphians— it's not even listed in the Yellow Pages—is Strolli's (1528 Dickinson Street); cheap, good, homey, good, southern

Italian, good. We'll also confess an unreasonable affection for the dining room at the Barclay. Sure, it's expensive, and the food has a habit of arriving overcooked, but where else can you see all those characters from *The Philadelphia Story* sipping gibsons in Georgian splendor?

High Culture. The Academy of Music is America's best concert hall, both acoustically and aesthetically. The Philadelphia Orchestra suffers, perhaps, from the romantic soul of Eugene Ormandy, yet few orchestras can match its shimmering technical polish. Two local opera companies—the Grand and the Lyric—perform periodically at the Academy of Music, as do the Philadelphia Civic Ballet and the Pennsylvania Ballet.

Theater's a letdown. After a brief flowering in the early sixties, repertory slipped to summer-stock level. That leaves Philadelphians at the mercy of occasional pre-Broadway efforts, touring companies, and an uneven local company called the Drama Guild.

Low Culture. Pennsylvania's Blue Laws go a long way toward explaining the origin of the Philadelphia joke. Common sense and common thirst have triumphed in recent years, however, so alcohol can be served until 2:00 a.m. on Saturday night, and it's even possible to wet your whistle on the sabbath. Gray-flannel-suit buffs like the Chinese-modern bar at the Barclay, so authentic that it's called a "cocktail lounge." At the Penthouse, thirty-three stories above Locust Street, you'd swear you were in San Francisco (or Seattle or Denver or Kansas City), save for the view of Philadelphia's muscle, the great oil refineries clustered along the Delaware.

Authentic nightclubs are mostly over in the New Jersey suburbs, the better to serve the Eydie Gormé–texturized polyester–Ford LTD crowd. (Try the Latin Casino in

158

nearby Cherry Hill.) Center City has good jazz, though, at Just Jazz, cabaret entertainment at the Bijou Café, two sophisticated discothèques (Cobblestones, Fast Eddie's), and at least one lowlife bar (Frank's) that tolerates strangers.

• THE BEST WEEKEND GETAWAY WITHIN ONE HUNDRED MILES OF . . .

Boston

In summer, skip the hustle of Cape Cod or Nantucket for the Victorian calm of Wentworth-by-the-Sea, a few miles south of Portsmouth, New Hampshire. From the barest description, the Wentworth might be just another oversized adult summer camp: eighteen-hole golf course, Olympic-sized swimming pool, tennis courts, horseback riding, nightly dancing, weekly clambake. It is big (250 rooms) and it does offer enough activities to soothe the spirits of the manic.

But the Wentworth is special. The stately white buildings are scattered over acres of heavily landscaped grounds, a few hundred yards from the sea. Rooms are large enough to breathe in and are furnished with taste: some have terraces overlooking the water, others are in cottages above the beach. There's no regimentation here, no waiting in line for a turn at the buffet, no rudeness born of anonymity from the staff. Unlike most resorts, the Wentworth is best in high season (July and August); late spring and early fall, you may bump into a wholesale hardware dealers' convention or a pre-season pep rally for pizza franchisers.

The rest of the year, consider the pleasures of southern New Hampshire from the vantage point of the John Hancock Inn. Freezing fall nights in the densely wooded hills around Hancock (New Hampshire) yield about the prettiest autumn foliage this side of an American Heritage coffee-table book. Mid-December brings reliable snow cover to the local ski areas, Onset and Crotched Mountain. Cross-country skiing is also catching on here, with a half-

dozen trail networks to choose from. Use the late-spring hiatus between waves of tourists to explore a region that has escaped the ravages of covered-mall shopping centers and twenty-four-hour-a-day electronic banking.

The inn itself has fifteen rooms, each busy with Americana. The food is perhaps the best in lower New Hampshire: hearty New England, with occasional intrusions of James Beard. And if you happen to be there for lunch in the spring, be sure to reserve a table on the enclosed patio.

Denver

No grand resort on the order of the Broadmoor in Colorado Springs, the C Lazy U Ranch offers pleasures less formal. This solid lodge on the edge of Rocky Mountain National Park (Granby, Colorado) specializes in horseback riding, with trails leading into the deep wilderness of the park and surrounding national forest. If long days in the saddle don't appeal, the C Lazy U has tennis, a heated pool, a trout-stocked lake, and endless meadowlands for hiking and cross-country skiing.

Lodge accommodations are one cut up from motel modern. No room service, but food and drink appropriate to the setting—steaks, barbeques, and so forth. The best seasons are June and September, when the weather's good and the tourists aren't out in force.

Phoenix

Arizona specializes in posh desert resorts. Around Phoenix, choose among the Arizona Biltmore, Wigwam, Camelback Inn, Rancho Los Caballeros. Choose, that is, if you reserve months in advance and tuck away the requisite sixty to seventy dollars per person, per night for high-season room and vittles.

For a weekend free of glitter and BMW's with California

plates, try the Hermosa Inn at Paradise Valley. This small hotel manages the standard tennis courts, pool, and desert views. Unlike nearby giants, however, it also offers serenity. The architecture is upper-class Latin hacienda: cool colors, whitewashed walls, planted courtyards. Rooms and villas are spread out over the property, isolated from the dining room and lobby. The Hermosa revs up a bit during the winter, but drifts along sleepily the rest of the year.

New York

Mohonk Mountain House is surely the most unlikely resort in North America. Less hotel than capital of a wilderness kingdom, the great barnlike structure perches uncomfortably on the shores of Lake Mohonk near New Paltz. surrounded by 7,500 acres of private forest land. Actually, the architecture, a sort of New World version of the Château de Chambord, grows on you. And even if you never learn to love its jumble of turrets and gables, Mohonk has other charms. In summer there's horseback riding, canoeing, swimming, backpacking, tennis, golf. In winter, try skiing (cross-country and Alpine), skating, or afternoon tea in the grand parlor.

Mohonk House is the legacy of the Smiley family. They still own the resort—the forest land is a charitable trust—so guests must accept certain family idiosyncrasies: to be specific, restricted drinking hours and no smoking in the public rooms. Clean living doesn't slow the place down much; Mohonk attracts a crowd as eclectic as the architecture: 50 percent Bloomingdale's, 50 percent L. L. Bean.

P.S. Specify in advance if your life is incomplete without private plumbing. All Mohonk's rooms are pleasant, but less fortunate tenants must seek comforts at the end of the hall.

Los Angeles

This is lotusland, all right. But the money is at least third-decade, if not third-generation: Sevilles outnumber Eldorados by five to one. The Santa Barbara Biltmore exudes elegance, a bastion of luxury on twenty landscaped acres by the Pacific. It's a large establishment—190 rooms—yet size is painless here. The Biltmore runs efficiently in spite of the sprawl, and the inevitable lack of intimacy provides psychological cover against unsolicited intrusions.

Accommodations and food rate a solid A. No two rooms are alike, though all meet the rigorous standards of the Biltmore's Holmby Hills clientele. Most have balconies or patios with a good view of the bay or of the Santa Ynez mountains to the north. The hotel maintains a pool and private beach; guests in search of other diversions may obtain club privileges for golf, tennis, and riding. In keeping with its image, the Biltmore's kitchen is conservative—heavy on prime ribs, light on garlic. But what prime ribs . . .

Seasons don't mean much; the hotel is nearly always full. But you're more likely to get a room on short notice during the spring and fall.

San Francisco

Cheat a little on distance. After all, what's an extra twenty miles when the destination is the Del Monte Lodge on the Monterey Peninsula? The lodge is within the Del Monte forest, a 5,000-acre private playground for the scourge of the working classes, on what may be the most beautiful coast in the United States. Rooms face either the Pebble Beach golf course or Carmel Bay and the mountains.

Guests without a passion for the links (there are two nasty eighteen-hole courses and an easy nine-holer) may find amusement at the pool or tennis club. The lodge also has riding stables, should you care to explore the Del Monte woodlands on horseback. Two dining rooms serve similar food, country-club bountiful at breakfast and lunch, elaborate French at dinner. When the kitchen aims *haute,* it doesn't quite deliver. But this is a mere quibble.

Plan far ahead for reservations any time of the year, and don't bother trying during the Bing Crosby Pro-Am.

Washington

The Mobil Guide awards five stars to the Tides Inn and Golf Lodge (Irvington, Virginia). But don't hold it against the place. This is no made-in-Hollywood extravaganza with bathroom phones and his and hers wet bars. The image is more a cross between old-fashioned Virginia hospitality and bourgeois European comfort. All confused, to be sure, by the Scots-plaid decorative motif chosen to honor Sir Guy Campbell, the designer of the Tides' golf course.

The Tides is one of the comfiest places on the East Coast to do nothing in particular. Sit around on the little beach, check out the cabin cruisers docked at the marina, stuff down a seafood lunch on board the hotel's power yacht while cruising the Rappahannock River. Or, if the sloth of it all overwhelms, play tennis, rent a sailboat, swim laps in the pool, embarrass yourself on the narrow fairways.

A full house—standard from May to September—doesn't strain the service. The best seasons, however, are spring and fall, when the weather is cooler.

• THE BEST WINE CELLAR

What you put in it is your businsss; we mean the best place

to bring young wines to maturity and keep old ones on the right side of senility.

By far the most important requirement for a good cellar is cool, constant temperature: the ideal is 53 to 57 degrees F. Fluctuations down to 40 degrees or up to 75 won't turn Bordeaux to wine vinegar overnight, but if you cannot control the temperature fairly rigidly it's a waste of good grapes to store the stuff for very long. "Very long" for whites means a few months; reds can manage about a year if they're kept below room temperature.

Darkness, humidity, and air circulation also make a difference. Aging depends upon delicate chemical changes, which are disturbed by light, so whatever else your cellar has, it must also have a door. Given enough time, dryness destroys bottle corks. Hence, unless you are keen to recork your wines every year, humidity must be controlled. Stale air is almost as bad as dry air over the long pull, since smells eventually seep through the slightly porous cork.

Over-the-hill refrigerators as mini-cellars strike out on humidity and circulation but can still lengthen the life of good wine. If you do use a refrigerator, be sure to limit storage to the part of the box that can maintain that constant 53 to 57 degrees; the veggie keeper is usually 15 degrees warmer than the top shelf.

Last on the list of requirements is peace and quiet. Sloshing wine around seems to age it in an unpleasant way. This is supposedly why some light European wines end up dull and raisiny by the time they reach Baltimore harbor. The real reason has more to do with the chemicals and extra alcohol added to export wines to give them longer commercial shelf life. In any event, common sense suggests keeping wine away from road or machine vibration and organizing the cellar so you don't have to move bottles much to read their labels.

The best cellars around are thirty feet underground, natural caves used by big shippers in Beaune, France. Chances are excellent that any older Burgundy you purchased ready to drink grew up there. If you aren't lucky enough to own an old farmhouse with a deep, damp cellar, the practical options for storing wine well are limited. A few cities have commercial wine-storage warehouses that sell space to individual investors. But before you trust your 1970 Château Latour to one, see how close it comes to the real thing.

Another possibility is a specially built wine vault. The Universal-Viking Company of Hempstead, New York, manufactures air-conditioned, hardwood-lined boxes for the purpose, with capacities ranging from 156 to 2,028 bottles. Cool air and water vapor are expensive *chez* Universal-Viking: vaults retail for $1,500 to $5,000. Naturally, the Universal-Viking Wine Vault is sold by Hammacher Schlemmer in New York. They'd be happy to gift-wrap.

Sour grapes postscript: If you want to impress your friends, drop the wine-cellar idea, and collect first editions or memorize the names of the Arab emirates or something. It rarely pays to age your own, as anyone who caught the bug in the late sixties or early seventies knows too well; Château Lafite '70 sells today for half the going rate in 1974. Even if rising prices cover your storage costs, there's lost interest on the investment to consider. Sure, a $5 bottle purchased now might be worth $8 in seven years. But $5 in an 8 percent savings certificate will be worth $8.57 seven years later. And savings banks give away toasters.

THE BEST . . .

ACKNOWLEDGMENTS

My thanks to Jim Albrecht, Aaron Asher, Ben Calabrese, Chris Casson, Akosh Chernush, Kay Chernush, Elaine Chubb, Gene Colice, Don Cutler, Charles Gerson, Mary-Joan Gerson, Bernie Glassman, Judy Hébert, Peter Kornman, Myer Kutz, Susan Lee, Nancy Meiselas, Rhoma Mostel, Barbara Neilson, David Previant, Lois Previant, Lennie Ross, David Schwartz, Nancy Seastrom, Cynthia Shafto, Bill Smith, Emmy Smith, Luisa Smith, Nell Smith, Tom Stewart, Cynthia White.